Working with Black Adult Learners

A Practical Guide

Stella Dadzie

National Institute of Adult Continuing Education

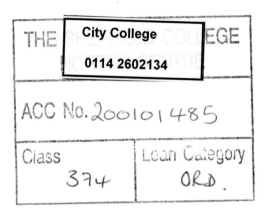
Published by the National Institute of Adult Continuing Education (England and Wales)
21 De Montfort Street, Leicester LE1 7GE
Company registration no. 2603322
Charity registration no. 1002775

First published 1993
Reprinted 1994

Cataloguing in Publication Data
A CIP record for this book is available from the British Library

ISBN 1 872941 34 6

Printed and bound in Great Britain by Biddles Ltd, Guildford and King's Lynn

CONTENTS

Section 1: Pre-Course

Section 2: Recruitment and Selection

Section 3: On-Course

FOREWORD

At NIACE's July 1991 Ethnic Minorities Education Policy Committee (EMEPC) conference in Bradford delegates were invited to consider a range of themes relating to good practice as it affects black and other ethnic and linguistic minority adult learners. The aims of the conference included the production of a set of recommendations on what constitutes good practice with black adult learners. Participants, whose experience spanned adult, community, further, higher and voluntary sector education, examined a variety of issues. Their discussions focused on:

- language support
- anti-racist strategies
- multi-culturalism
- relations with employers
- progression routes
- outreach strategies
- on-course support
- assessment and accreditation of prior learning/overseas qualifications
- curriculum issues.

This practical guide has been developed as a result of this recommendation and subsequent workshops organised by EMEPC in April and July 1992. It draws on my own work as a specialist trainer in this area, and on the growing body of expertise and good practice which has been developed in the delivery of education and training to black adult learners. It will serve as a useful resource for those who work 'at the chalk-face' of such provision as well as for those who develop and seek to implement equal opportunities and anti-racist policies.

The sheer diversity of potential needs, issues and learning contexts precludes the production of a definitive resource. However, this book is a first step towards a focus for consultation, training and the confident implementation of good practice in this crucial and often undervalued area of education provision.

ACKNOWLEDGEMENTS

Members of NIACE's Ethnic Minorities Education Policy Committee, in particular Joan Carter-Graham, Zahid Hamid, Nelson Kachisi, Ella Lutchmayer, Kanwal Pattar, Shamin Rehman, Phyllis Thompson.

Workshop participants who took part in EMEPC's July 1991 Conference, Bradford; NIACE's April 1992 Conference, Nottingham; EMEPC's July 1992 Conference, Birmingham.

Others who have offered invaluable suggestions, advice and examples of good practice, in particular Toni Fazaeli, Leicestershire Community Education; Inder Gera; Ahmed Gurnah, Education Officer, SUMES; Derek Hooper, Wandsworth Adult College; Marion Molteno, Croydon ESOL Service and ALBSU; Parvin Paidar, World University Service; Gulshen Reif, The College of North-East London; Bharati Ruwala, Newham Community College; Margaret Henry for her meticulous proof-reading.

For permission to reproduce material we are grateful to the following:

Afro-Caribbean People in Leicestershire Research Project; Birkbeck College, University of London; Bournville College of Further Education; The British Council; College of North East London; Croydon Continuing Education and Training Service; Hackney Adult Education Institute; Hackney Community College; Islington Education Advice Service for Adults; Islington Federal College; The Moat Centre, Highfields, Leicester; Newham Community College; University of East London; Wandsworth Adult College; World University Service.

WHY FOCUS ON BLACK ADULT LEARNERS?

Developments over the past decade have shown conclusively that those educational practices and opportunities which were intended to promote equality of opportunity have, if properly embedded, proved to be in the interests of all learners.

Nowhere is this more evident than in the varied and innovative responses around the country to the needs of black adult learners. The growth of Access provision, for example, has persuaded many higher education providers to target and accommodate not only black students, but mature students generally. Community outreach strategies, too, have encouraged a more consultative, responsive approach to the development of provision to meet the needs of all sectors of the community.

However, the desire to promote and embed good practice is not the only motive for producing this book. Available statistical data confirm that there is an urgent and growing need to improve education and training opportunities for black adult learners. For example:

- the 1990 Labour Force Survey, which reveals that levels of unemployment among both unskilled and highly-qualified blacks are up to 60% higher; and that only 62% of people from ethnic minorities aged between 16 and 24 are economically active, compared with 85% of their white counterparts
- current demographic indicators, which predict a significant increase in young black adults of working age to 8% of the workforce (compared to 4.5% of the general population)
- the marked demographic decline among 16–19-year-olds (from 1.05 million in 1980 to 0.65 million by the year 2000) which will require employers to depend increasingly on black workers, women and other economically marginalised groups, or recruit European labour to make up the shortfall.

Recent social changes have also highlighted the need to defend and expand education and training opportunities for black adult learners, particularly in a climate of resurgent racism. Examples can be seen in Britain's new status within the European Community post-1992. This threatens to entrench black unemployment by increasing competition from (white) Europeans, and encouraging legislation designed to limit the movement, rights and entitlements of Europe's ethnic minorities. There has also been a growth in the number of refugees, which has rapidly increased the need for more responsive ESOL provision to cater for a diversity of language, learning and accreditation needs, and for more efficient guidance, community networking and referral systems.

In the education system, the onus is now on education managers to ensure that available provision is cost-effective, while at the same time demonstrating a responsiveness to community needs. This requirement has proved a difficult and often contradictory mission, inhibited by budget cuts and a curtailment of the powers of LEAs to resource and enforce equal opportunities policies. As a consequence, many relevant projects and initiatives are being closed or curtailed, resulting not only in a loss of much-needed services, but also in a haemorrhage of vital professional expertise.

Financial delegation and the new further and higher education corporations have fuelled concerns within black communities about the continued local accountability of institutions forced to prioritise income-bearing and profit-generating courses with readily 'measurable' results. Many black adult learners have benefited from subsidised, '21-hour' or non-certificated learning opportunities, with less tangible or measurable outcomes such as increased confidence or clearer progression options. Should courses such as these be deemed unprofitable or difficult to justify in the present economic climate, the consequences for black adults and other vulnerable groups in the community are unthinkable.

There is no room for complacency in such a context. The need has never been greater for those who are committed to access and equality of opportunity to consolidate those services and practices which have been most effective in challenging discrimination and racism, and to promote a better understanding of the processes which gave rise to them.

Aims

☐ To identify key issues and provide examples of good practice in the delivery of education and training to black adult learners.

☐ To suggest ideas, guidelines and resources for the implementation of achievable anti-racist strategies.

☐ To provide a focus for training and consultation for anti-racist education workers and others seeking personal and institutional commitment to positive action.

Target Audience

☐ Lecturers, teachers, tutors and trainers working with black adult learners in post-16 education and the voluntary sector.

☐ Managers and policy-makers responsible for the promotion, delivery and/or evaluation of education and training for black adult learners.

☐ Members of governing bodies and Training and Enterprise Councils concerned with adult continuing education in further, higher, community and adult education.

Making the Best Use of this Book

Each section is structured to include:

☐ introductory comments to clarify current thinking and contextualise recommended good practice. Use this to stimulate discussion and debate in working parties, course team meetings, staff development workshops and other consultation and training forums

☐ an outline, in checklist form, of some of the key issues for students, practitioners and managers (as appropriate). Use these checklists as a training aide, or to inform planning, review and policy development discussions

☐ a practical example, case study or resource. Use this to illustrate good practice or to generate critical discussion as a basis for staff and curriculum development

☐ a list of resources and useful contacts. Use these as a training and induction resource, and to assist the development of individual awareness or wider networks.

Terminology Used

Adult Learners

This term encompasses the diverse group of learners in post-compulsory, voluntary or statutory education seeking to develop or update their skills, knowledge and/or competence for their own professional, vocational, social or personal development.

Bilingual

Unless otherwise stated, references to the language needs of bi- or multi-lingual adults include speakers of Patois who, because of the distinctive nature of languages in the Caribbean, may also require language support or mother-tongue provision.

Black

This is a generic term used throughout to refer to those who are identifiably different from the ethnic majority because of race, colour, ethnic origin, language, religion or culture. The term encompasses:

- black people born overseas who have settled in Britain
- British-born or second generation black adults of Afri-Caribbean and Asian origin
- asylum-seekers and refugees
- overseas students
- members of religious and linguistic minority communities.

Despite a diversity of educational needs and circumstances, black adults share a common experience of institutional racism which may result in discrimination, harassment or marginalisation within the education system.

Because black adult learners are not an homogenous group, acknowledging what they have in common should not detract from our recognition of the diversity of religious, cultural, linguistic and social needs within 'minority' communities or the need to challenge personal and institutional stereotypes by responding to black adult learners as individuals. (See also Appendix 1.)

Course

In the interests of conciseness, course is used to refer to the full range of available education, training and study programmes, encompassing:

- discrete and modular provision
- formal and informal learning
- full- and part-time courses
- institution-based, work-based and community-based learning
- flexible and open learning.

Institution

This term is used as a means of acknowledging institutional racism. It encompasses colleges and universities, as well as all the voluntary, outreach, community and adult education projects which, although they may not be institution-based, are nevertheless responsible for examining their practices and procedures.

SECTION 1: PRE-COURSE

1.1 COMMUNITY CONSULTATION

Community consultation enables institutions to learn from local groups and individuals about their educational needs and aspirations, by establishing appropriate forums to evaluate their experience and expectations of available provision.

It has traditionally been most effective where the institution is actively involved in a dialogue with representative members of the different black communities and other groups it professes or aspires to serve.

This cannot take place without the human and material resources necessary to sustain the consultative process and ensure that suggestions are translated into action. Nor can it occur if the institution always presumes to take the leadership role.

Consultation should be a collaborative, two-way process – flexible enough to accommodate a range of approaches and viewpoints and broad enough to encourage genuine and equal communication between and within local communities. It can take place in a range of different contexts, both formal and informal, and should be underpinned by the explicit aim to draw on the untapped potential and expertise that exists within local black communities.

Making the institution's resources available to established community groups – and thereby demonstrating a readiness to give something back to the community in the form of classroom space or staff time and expertise – is one way of promoting a positive profile in the community and encouraging a sense of community ownership, both of which are prerequisites for any consultative activity.

Black staff who are bilingual or who already have strong links within their communities could prove to be an invaluable resource for consultation purposes. However, it is presumptuous to assume that they will automatically wish to represent the institution in this way, simply because they are black or speak one of the relevant community languages. They may well feel constrained by religious, social, cultural or political differences; by a reluctance to become professionally 'ghettoised'; by a lack of confidence; or, quite simply, by the weight of their other commitments.

The right of staff to choose – and to be appropriately compensated for – any extra-curricular community involvement, whether their role is consultative, representative or supportive, should be fully acknowledged by their managers.

Traditionally, language has posed a major barrier to education and training for those whose first language is not English. Whatever the forum or context for consultation, literacy or fluency in English should not be taken for granted. To put non-English speakers at their ease and encourage a genuine dialogue, mother-tongue speakers or interpreters should be present where needed.

Once contacts with individuals and groups within local communities are established, they should be encouraged to continue, whether formally or informally. This means making active efforts to sustain networks and ensure that staff's consultative functions are properly embedded, for example by including them prominently within the academic calendar, staff appraisal criteria, course aims and relevant job descriptions.

Institutions which profess to seek the community's views must first gain the community's trust and respect. This is a long-term investment, involving a commitment of both time and effort. If the people who are being consulted feel they have not been given a voice, or that their ideas have been ignored or misrepresented, it is unlikely that they will take the exercise – or the institution – very seriously.

The development of efficient monitoring, feedback and evaluation procedures to ensure that the institution 'hears' and respects what local black people are saying and is seen to be responsive to their needs is therefore fundamental to successful consultation.

Community Consultation Strategies

- ☐ Recognise and distinguish between self-appointed, informal and elected representatives.
- ☐ Raise awareness of what the institution has to offer by establishing contacts with staff and users of:
  - cultural and religious centres
  - Saturday schools
  - community language classes
  - voluntary organisations
  - ethnic minority shops/businesses
  - self-help groups
  - community centres
  - youth clubs.
- ☐ Organise public meetings, open days, radio phone-ins and street polls to find out what local people think of the institution, and what they'd like to see happen there.
- ☐ Encourage constructive suggestions and criticisms via course reviews, student evaluations, written or oral surveys and questionnaires.
- ☐ Encourage mutual involvement in relevant committees, community networks and specialist working parties.
- ☐ Establish mechanisms to facilitate regular feedback from internal/external guidance workers and staff involved in outreach work.
- ☐ Encourage staff attendance at community meetings, campaign meetings, festivals and celebrations.
- ☐ Tap into existing community forums by encouraging staff to join management committees, special interest groups, and informal or voluntary networks.
- ☐ Set up and/or service community forums to look at local education and training issues and identify needs and ways of meeting them.
- ☐ Exchange ethnic monitoring data and be prepared to discuss implications.
- ☐ Be honest about any gaps or weaknesses in existing provision.
- ☐ Be prepared to accept criticism and to address the genuine fears and perceptions others in the community may have.

The campaign and the community infrastructure

Community Steering Groups have been set up in order to enable the communities involved in the campaign to monitor their own progress and more effectively participate in decision-making. These groups are shaping the future of the campaign and of their community. A community representative on the management group describes what is happening thus:

For the first time the community is dealing face to face with colleges. Sometimes we agree and at other times we disagree, but the steering groups and the management groups of the campaign are the framework for our discussions. This is the way education should be conducted. Educational institutions should be accountable to us (Said Ali).

Elected members of the Yemeni community include the literacy campaign as a regular agenda item in their meetings. Some communities discuss existing developments, while others move beyond that.

The campaign has become a vehicle for discussing common issues within the black community. Steering groups are pursuing the general interests of the black community and challenge the notion that their needs are marginal. It is certainly evident that black communities are looking for ways to enhance and develop further community control of learning.

Recently all black communities got together to set up the Black Community Forum. It is hoped that this initiative will bring black communities together to discuss major issues and reach collective political positions...

Figure 1.1 Extract from *Adults Learning* April 1992, a special issue on the Sheffield Black Literacy Campaign

... As a result, the colleges are also gaining a wealth of cultural knowledge by increasing their understanding of these communities. But through working with the campaigns, colleges are also subsequently improving service delivery and increasing their FTEs.

The community supported the campaign through public meetings, the use of their premises and transport, by participating in the recruitment process, attending and chairing management group meetings, and creating access into places of worship and other community focal points. An important outcome of their involvement has been the way women have led and developed the campaign.

Their role has developed from a position of isolation to a position of strength. Women had previously regarded colleges as inappropriate. Learners found a platform in the campaign through which they could take charge of their education. Most of the women who joined the campaign have since developed meaningful routes into employment or further education.

One women assistant described her experience in this way:

My parents made me finish school at 16. I did not pass any exams. Community representatives came to see my parents about the Literacy Campaign, and succeeded in persuading them to allow me to apply as an Assistant. It was very satisfying for me to be working for my community and the experience I gained has equipped me to find employment. I hope to make a contribution to the development of my community (Safia).

Figure 1.1 (continued)

COMMUNITY CONSULTATION

Issues for Local Communities

- What is the character, ethos, purpose and location of this institution?
- How does it operate? Who pays for it? Who uses it?
- What potential is there for us to influence what it does?
- Why should we believe that this is a genuine attempt to establish a dialogue with us?
- Are there any staff from our own ethnic background with whom we could talk? Can they 'speak our language'?
- Who makes the decisions? Will they get to hear our views?
- How seriously will they take our suggestions, and our criticisms? Will they act upon them?
- Is the provision accessible to our community in terms of its location, the provision of language support and the nature, level and entry requirements of the courses?
- Is the institution willing to respond to our particular socio-economic circumstances, and any dietary, cultural and religious needs?

COMMUNITY CONSULTATION

Issues for Practitioners

- Which members of the local black communities should our institution/area of provision be able to attract?
- How will we establish and maintain a dialogue with:
  - individuals and groups?
  - elected and informal representatives?
  - community organisations and their spokespersons?
- Can we tap into any existing community networks or forums?
- Have we taken account of the the full range of views within local communities, including differences within each group based on class, gender, religion, age, language, etc.?
- Do we have a clear idea of what we hope to gain from our consultation efforts?
- How will we reconcile conflicting or competing demands?
- What procedures exist for feedback, evaluation and implementation of the ideas and opinions expressed?

COMMUNITY CONSULTATION

Issues for Managers

- What human and material resources have we identified to support this area of work?
- What do available ethnic monitoring data reveal about the ethnicity and location of our potential and actual clients?
- Are there any groups in our catchment or particular postal areas who are over- or under-represented within the institution or on specific courses? Do we know why?
- What formal or informal links with local communities has this institution already established? Which have been most successful?
- What kind of local contacts have been most effective as a means of identifying educational needs and vocational aspirations? (Can we learn from other local providers?)
- Shouldn't a (bilingual?) member of staff from the same ethnic group be involved in this area of work? Can we appoint someone or second an existing member of staff?
- What should we do to ensure genuine and respresentative community involvement in our decision-making processes?
- Are the communities we serve fully represented on our Governing Body?
- What procedures or mechanisms can we use to ensure that any issues raised are given full and formal consideration, particularly for course planning and evaluation purposes?
- How can we ensure that any staff involved in consultation work are credited for what they do and fully involved in the development and/or delivery of relevant provision?

Resources

Access to FE for Black Adults
FEU, 1988

Anti-Racist Strategies in College and Community
FEU, 1989

Literacy for a Change, a special issue of NIACE's monthly journal *Adults Learning* on the Sheffield Black Literacy Campaign
April 1992

Black Community Access: A Development Paper
UDACE, 1990

Learning for a Purpose: Participation in education and training by adults from ethnic minorities
Naomi Sargant, NIACE, 1993

Useful Contacts

Local Community Relations and Racial Equality Councils

Local Voluntary Action/Voluntary Services Organisations

Local Community, Welfare, Refugee and Religious groups

Local Tenants' Groups and Campaign Organisations

Local Adult Education Providers

Local Saturday/Supplementary Schools

Local Community Language Classes

Local Community Centres

Local Economic Development Unit

Local TEC (Training and Enterprise Council)

Community representatives on local school and college governing bodies and voluntary management committees.

1.2 POLICY DEVELOPMENT

The existence of an anti-racist policy serves as a declared commitment to institutional change and adds weight to what might otherwise be no more than the good intentions of a few committed or well-meaning individuals. It is the means by which an institution can make explicit and public its contract with its black staff, students and the wider community, as outlined in its mission statement. With no such contract in place, developments tend to take place in isolation, do not inform strategic planning or resource prioritisation and may therefore lack credibility and coherence.

The development of a comprehensive anti-racist policy can be seen as an essential first step towards the embedding of good, anti-discriminatory practice within the service or institution. Ideally it should be a free-standing policy in its own right, or a distinct and discrete part of a wider-ranging equal opportunities policy.

However, the production of an anti-racist policy is not an end in itself, nor will people take notice of it simply because it exists. Its development, planning and implementation should be regarded as a means of raising awareness and encouraging a sense of collective 'ownership'. This is possible only if it involves the widest consultation, particularly with the black students, staff and communities it is intended to benefit.

Policy development is best conducted via structured and focused discussions, involving both staff and students. These should be facilitated by a trainer or staff member with sufficient competence and sensitivity to handle the complex, uncomfortable issues that can arise when people are required to confront the need for personal and institutional change. Established committees, working parties, staff meetings, union meetings, student tutorials, and training or policy development workshops are all viable forums for consultation.

These should be conducted as widely as possible with:

- representatives of local black communities, including parents, voluntary organisations and the local Community Relations Council
- students from a diversity of backgrounds who represent the full range of courses
- teaching staff at all levels, including part-timers and sessional staff
- support staff at all levels, including reception, clerical and maintenance staff, technicians, caretakers
- and others who contribute to the provision of the service.

An anti-racist policy which fails to set clear targets or address the needs of both employees and clients of the service is destined to lack credibility. It should therefore cover all aspects of service delivery for both staff and students, and incorporate an action plan, identifying and naming who is responsible for the implementation, monitoring and evaluation of each key area.

MISSION STATEMENT

This College is dedicated to seeking out potential students, identifying their needs and developing life-long learning opportunities to meet them. The College meets the diverse needs of its students by ...

- providing lifelong learning opportunities for professional, vocational, social and personal development

- admissions without regard to formal entrance requirements

- competency assessment and the accreditation of prior experience and achievement

- life planning, delivered through vocational and educational guidance

- flexible scheduling of classes

- accessible locations for learning

- open, flexible and alternative learning modes

- courses of study to widen access to professional and educational opportunities

- opportunities to upgrade and develop new skills

- promoting equality and cultural enrichment

- personal and professional development

- ongoing student support

(With thanks to Colin Flint, Principal of Solihull College of Technology, a keynote speaker at NIACE's 1992 National Conference, whose outline of Rocklands Community College's Mission Statement (USA) provided the inspiration for this example.)

Figure 1.2 Anti-racism reflected in the mission statement

STUDENT RECRUITMENT AND ADMISSIONS

The College's student body should reflect the ethnic composition of the community it serves.

Action Plan

1. Course publicity and interviews will reassure all students that they will be welcomed to the College. This will involve maximum use of community and ethnic press.

2. Student admission requirements will not formally demand, or informally require, more or higher qualifications than the relevant examining/validating bodies define. Any necessary additional qualification must be within the scope/experience of all students.

3. All admission tests are submitted to the Principal to be reviewed in terms of their content and language, to ensure that they test student ability, not culturally specific knowledge.

4. An information pack/booklet in a range of languages on processes and strategies of becoming and being a student will be on offer.

5. The College will continue to make use of resources in the community in order to provide bilingual support and translation during advice, recruitment and selection procedures.

6. There will continue to be liaison with employers, community workers and careers officers, to ensure that students from ethnic minority groups come forward for all courses.

7. Statistics on the ethnic origins of students will continue to be kept by course teams. Their subsequent progress should be monitored.

8. Anti-racist staff development for reception staff and all those involved in recruitment will be provided.

9. Some aspects of the validation of overseas qualifications and the currency of UK qualifications abroad need to be clarified in collaboration with the British Council.

Figure 1.3 Extract from Hackney College Anti-Racist Policy

POLICY DEVELOPMENT

Issues for Students

- Does this anti-racist policy have any teeth?
- Are there black staff at all levels within the organisation? Where are they concentrated? Do they appear to be benefiting from the policy?
- Does the policy cover all the relevant areas, including:
  - my right to equal access to buildings, courses and services?
  - my right to a curriculum that takes account of my prior learning, my cultural heritage and my language and learning needs?
  - my right to personal support and counselling which is both culturally relevant and culturally sensitive?
  - my right to have recourse to fair and equitable disciplinary and grievance procedures, should I be the target or instigator of a complaint?
  - my need for an institutional ethos and learning environment which respects and reflects my own and others' cultural and religious orientation?

- What redress is available to me if the policy is not enforced? Are there clearly-stated procedures for lodging any grievances or complaints?

- Does the anti-racist policy have cross-institutional status and active managerial support?
- Do we have the staff and resources necessary to implement it?
- Do my own experiences and observations, and those of my colleagues, confirm that it is being actively implemented?
- Do we have access to relevant ethnic monitoring data for planning and review purposes?
- Do the data cover all the relevant areas, including:

STAFF RECRUITMENT AND SELECTION

- staff recruitment criteria which are not discriminatory and value bilingualism, overseas equivalent qualifications and transferrable skills
- objective selection and interviewing procedures
- clear, culturally unbiased job specifications

CURRICULUM RESOURCES

- availability of up-to-date, positive, relevant research and materials for curriculum planning
- adequate time for individuals and course teams to develop a non-Eurocentric, anti-racist syllabus

PERSONAL AND PROFESSIONAL DEVELOPMENT

- entitlement to fair, non-hierarchical appraisal
- entitlement to induction, personal/staff development and professional support
- equitable promotion opportunities which take account of potential, aptitude, competence and transferrable skills

ACCESS TO RELEVANT TRAINING

- commitment to an ongoing programme of staff development and training in issues relevant to the implementation of the policy

DISCIPLINARY AND GRIEVANCE PROCEDURES

- fair and explicit procedures which take acts of racism, and discrimination seriously and include the right to appeal.

POLICY DEVELOPMENT

Issues for Managers

- Is the policy a prominent feature of the institution's mission statement, its contract and working relations with students and staff and its strategic planning processes?
- Are we committed to turning our anti-racist rhetoric into reality by means of active, carefully monitored strategies for its implementation and a realistic budget allocation?
- What human and material resources have we identified to support the policy's implementation?
- Does our management information base include course-specific information about the number of black applicants, examination passes, course drop-out and post-course destinations?
- What do we do with this information? Is it used to plan provision, improve services and enhance progression opportunities?
- Is the existence of the policy evident in every aspect of the institution's practice, provision and ethos?
- Are there any areas in which staff are particularly resistant to change?
- Do we encourage applications from black staff who are representative of the communities within our catchment area?
- Do we value the input and encourage the professional development of any existing black staff?

- Does the policy cover all aspects of our students' learning experience, including:
  - **access** (admissions, recruitment, selection, interviewing, guidance and assessment)
  - **curriculum offer** (course content, study skills and learning support)
  - **language policy** (covering student admissions, the learning syllabus, classroom methodology, student support, assessment and accreditation)
  - **counselling, personal support and educational/vocational guidance** (availability of pre- and on-course guidance, tutorial support and [mother-tongue] counselling, if needed)
  - **disciplinary and grievance procedures** (access to procedures which are fair, explicit and rigorously applied)
  - **institutional ethos and environment** (respect for religious/cultural needs, promotion of positive, non-Eurocentric images)
- Is our policy

  COMPREHENSIVE
  - does it include all the relevant areas for staff, students, employers, assessors and the wider community?

  PART OF AN EXPLICIT CONTRACT
  - have we taken steps to ensure that equality of opportunity and access are part of our mission statement and our stated contract with all black staff and students?

  ACTION PLAN-FOCUSED
  - does it incorporate an action plan for each key area and specify which individuals are responsible for implementing, monitoring and evaluating it?
  - does it set targets?

  POSITIVE
  - does it stress the desired benefits of good equal opportunities/anti-racist practice to all students and staff and to the wider community served?

  REALISABLE
  - does it commit the necessary staff, training resources, budget allocation and review strategies required for its implementation?

ADEQUATELY RESOURCED

-   have we explored existing mainstream budgets and other funding possibilities in order to identify from the outset how aspects of the policy are to be resourced and embedded?
-   are relevant courses, projects, posts, services and initiatives adequately protected from the insecurities of short-term funding or virement arrangements?

REGULARLY REVIEWED?

-   do we update and amend the policy to ensure that it remains relevant?
-   do we encourage staff to meet regularly within course teams where they can take proper account of all aspects of the policy when developing and reviewing provision?

Resources

FE in Black and White
FEU, 1987

Planning NAFE: *Equal Opportunities for Ethnic Minorities*
FEU, 1988

Words or Deeds? (Review of Equal Opportunities Policies in Higher Education)
CRE, 1989

Staff Development for a Multi-Cultural Society (particularly Section 2, Unit 1: Policy)
FEU, 1988

Quality Education and Training for the Adult Unemployed: A Manual for Planners and Managers in Further Education
FEU REPLAN, 1992

Useful Contacts

Commission for Racial Equality, Eliot House, London SW1 5EH. Tel: 071 828 7022

Local Community Relations and Race Equality Council

EMEPC (Ethnic Minorities Education Policy Committee), c/o NIACE, 19B De Montfort St, Leicester LE1 7GE

Local organisations and providers with similar client groups and/or policy objectives to your own.

1.3 OUTREACH

Outreach is the process by which an institution takes itself out into the community in order to identify and work with those who are unrepresented (or under-represented) within its client group.

The purpose of outreach is to increase community participation by demonstrating a willingness to listen, adapt and be responsive to the needs of those who have not had access to traditional provision. This may be due to local perceptions or misgivings about the nature and requirements of available opportunities; or because of institutional barriers posed by inadequate language and learning support, financial constraints, location, lack of childcare, inflexible modes of delivery or a traditional 'take it or leave it' approach on the part of the provider.

Black communities are unlikely to have access to the same information about education and training opportunities as their white counterparts. They may lack the necessary confidence or knowledge of how to approach the institution, or they may simply perceive it as an unwelcoming or inappropriate learning environment. This is particularly true for refugees, asylum seekers and others who are likely to be socially, culturally or linguistically isolated, although it also applies to those who have been alienated by prior experiences of racism, neglect or marginalisation within the education system.

Consequently, outreach involves taking information about the service out into the community and, where appropriate, using non-institutional venues as a base for guidance work, informal groupwork or classes, thereby making the provision more appropriate and accessible. Ideally, it should involve a number of steps, designed to increase confidence and involvement gradually (see 'Stages of Outreach' below). It should be underpinned by a strong guidance element, relevant support, adequate resources and clear progression options. It should provide particular encouragement to those who would normally be excluded because of childcare responsibilities, financial or residential constraints, language or literacy barriers, cultural or religious requirements or lack of confidence.

Because outreach provision has proved most successful when developed *with* rather than *for* those it is intended to benefit, members of the targeted communities should be encouraged to become involved in all aspects of its planning and delivery. This includes control of activities and resources, as well as playing an active role in the development of courses that are relevant to their identified needs and interests.

Outreach work requires patience and sensitivity. The appointment of a competent outreach or community education worker with good relationships within the targeted community is therefore an essential first step. Because the outreach role is labour-intensive, requiring unconventional ways of working, evening and weekend work, informal contacts and home visits, it is essential that issues of institutional support – such as appropriate resources, working conditions, adequate supervision and access to appropriate training – are properly resolved.

The worker concerned needs to feel confident that s/he will be given sufficient managerial and material backing for any outreach initiatives, particularly those requiring institutional flexibility and innovation. To this end, clear lines of communication and mutual accountability need to be established between outreach workers, their managers and the black communities involved.

Above all, outreach workers need to be conscious of the meaning of advocacy, and of the dangers of disenfranchising the communities they work with by always presuming to speak on their behalf.

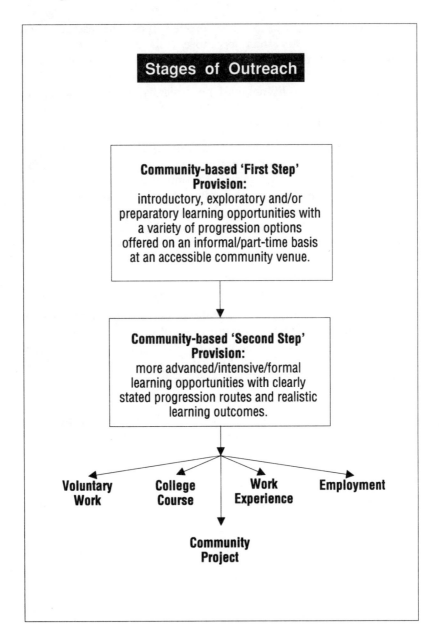

Figure 1.4 Stages of outreach

'My involvement this year with both statutory and voluntary organisations has taken the form of either committee membership, or one-off involvement to support certain ethnic minority events, or telephone contact. I have chosen those social, religious, cultural or leisure organisations which offer some educational elements to their members. Sometimes they are aware of their educational needs themselves and sometimes I assist them to see these needs. Education and training needs are considered both for the staff providing these services and the users.

I see no need at present to change this approach. My contacts with these organisations are over four years old. It is now a matter of keeping in contact with them, which takes less time that it took to establish them. I would, however, like to develop new relationships, and I intend to inform new community organisations that I can visit them and tell them about the college's Further and Adult Education provision...

I devote several hours a week to personal contact with ESOL clients referred either by themselves, their relatives, a voluntary organisation or the statutory sector. This part of my work is vital and essential, and without it the communities' needs could not be discovered...

The language class, which was set up at community centre A, is a combination of very young women with similar numbers of elderly and middle-aged women. Due to the emigration of some Bengali families within the last couple of years, we now have more Punjabi and Muslim women than Gujerati women... We have referred some of the overseas qualified women on to higher education classes in the College... The majority of the women are happy with two days of teaching, as most of them are housewives. Women who want more than this have been referred to the College...

The arrangement at community centre B seems to be quite successful too. The beginners' class has 22 on the register. We now have some Iranian and Bangladeshi women, which suggests a new influx into the Borough. We have increased the number of days from two to four at the request of the students and the tutor. It is going very well...'

(Extract from the outreach worker's report – Newham Community College/July 1991)

Figure 1.5 Establishing lines of communication with outreach workers

What Discourages Black Adult Learners From Taking Up Learning Opportunities?

A Checklist for Outreach Workers

- ☐ Inadequate or inappropriate information about what is available, including lack of information in community languages and lack of mother-tongue guidance.

- ☐ A belief that insufficient English, lack of qualifications, lack of money, age, dependents, etc. will hinder or prevent access.

- ☐ An assumption (often true) that the institution will not accredit prior learning or recognise overseas equivalent qualifications.

- ☐ A belief that the cost of studying will be too high, that benefits will be lost or that grants will not be available.

- ☐ Disillusionment with the education system, based on experiences of institutional racism or unemployment.

- ☐ Lack of familiarity with British educational culture and/or knowledge of how to negotiate the education system.

- ☐ The gap between actual needs (e.g. ESOL, financial support, childcare, preferred options) and available provision.

- ☐ The lack of women-only provision, facilities for women with young children or timetables that fit in with school hours.

- ☐ Inappropriate location and the cost and length of the journey involved.

- ☐ An unwelcoming ethos and environment, conveyed by staff attitudes, the state of buildings or an all-white student cohort.

- ☐ Fear of isolation.

- ☐ Poor guidance and reception facilities, including inappropriate attitudes and behaviour of security and reception staff.

- ☐ A monocultural ethos, reflected in an all or mainly white staff and a lack of appropriate religious, dietary or cultural facilities.

- ☐ Inflexible, inconvenient or inappropriate provision, including courses which enrol only once a year or do not take account of students' personal, domestic or work responsibilities.

- Can we trust the outreach worker(s)? Does s/he appear to understand our circumstances?
- What is s/he offering? Is there something we really need or could benefit from?
- Is s/he taking our views, experiences, circumstances and suggestions seriously?
- How much say will we have in determining the kind of learning activities on offer?
- What community resources can we draw on (e.g. places to meet, people who can act as mentors, interpreters, voluntary workers or home tutors, etc.)?
- Will any community-based outreach provision prove to be yet another form of under-resourced 'ghetto provision'?
- Will the course be accredited? Will it provide a route into employment, training, further or higher education for those of us who want one?
- If we progress to institution-based courses, will we continue to receive support or will we be left to sink or swim?

Issues for Practitioners

- Who are our actual and potential black students? Are they over- or under-represented on any of our courses? Do we know why?
- Are there any particular neighbourhoods, postal areas or groups (e.g. single parents, refugees, ex-prisoners) which we may need to target specifically?
- Which outreach strategies would be most appropriate? How are we to make and sustain our contacts?
- Are there any examples of previous or existing outreach work in the community which we can learn from? Who would know about them?
- Do the outreach worker(s) and staff who service outreach provision have sufficient knowledge of the needs, customs, skills, interests and languages of local communities?
- Which particular issues (e.g. language, cultural requirements, single-sex provision, accessibility of venue, etc.) will we need to take account of when planning and delivering outreach provision?
- How can we ensure that the communities' views, skills and resources are central to the outreach provision?
- Do the outreach workers have sufficient status, supervision, training and resources to perform their role effectively? Who are they accountable to within the institution?
- What support structures need to be in place to ensure that the outreach worker(s) are not isolated or marginalised?

Issues for Managers

- What human and material resources have we identified to support this area of work?
- Have we identified adequate accommodation, clerical support and an operational budget?
- Wouldn't a (bilingual?) outreach worker from the same ethnic group be more appropriate for this area of work?
- What training and support will s/he need?
- What do available data and research reveal about the educational needs, interests and priorities of local communities?
- How can we ensure that the outreach worker remains fully accountable both to the institution and to the communities s/he is working with?
- What procedures have we established to facilitate regular feedback, monitoring, evaluation and review of off-site provision?

THE GAZETTE
Friday, October 20, 1989

University steps out to greet the people

LONDON University is bringing education into the community with two new courses designed for adults who have few or no formal qualifications.

The university's extra-mural department, attached to Birkbeck College, is moving into Ealing this autumn and wants to cater for people who have little chance of moving on to higher education or improving their job prospects.

Tutors based at the Elthorne Site in Boston Road, Hanwell, will run courses in South Asian Studies and Community Health and Social Services.

The South Asian Studies course assumes some experience of studying and writing essays, though it will be open to everyone. The course will cover history, culture and politics.

The second course is for students interested in the health service or in voluntary care who need study guidance.

Jasbir Panesar, a development worker for London University, who has been working on the project with the health authority, Ealing social services and the education department, said: 'We are trying to get the whole community involved. We are bringing education home to the people.'

Figure 1.6 Bringing education to the community. Extract from the Brent and Ealing Gazette

Resources

Reaching Out: Further education and work in and with the community
REPLAN, May 1989

Outreach Work: Principles and policy
Rennie Johnston, Department of Adult Education, Training and Research, University of Southampton

Useful Contacts

Local Community Relations/Racial Equality Council

Local Voluntary Action/Voluntary Service Organisation

Local Community, Welfare, Refugee and Religious Groups

Tenants' Associations

Local schools and community centres

Local TECs and Jobcentres (for information about training and employment trends)

Open College Federation/Regional Networks (for information about course validation and accreditation)

Extra-Mural Studies, Adult Education, Continuing Education departments of local higher education providers (to explore possible franchising arrangements or collaborative projects)

1.4 MARKETING AND PUBLICITY

Effective marketing and publicity involves a readiness to identify potential clients, their needs, interests and aspirations, and to provide information about what the service can offer them, using a variety of methods and media.

A spot survey of students at enrolment is likely to reveal that a significant majority heard about the provision via word-of-mouth. This is especially true of students from bilingual communities, where people often depend on family and community grapevines for information, recommendations and warnings about local services.

This is partly due to a continuing reliance on oral traditions, particularly among refugees, recent arrivals, and people from countries where literacy levels are low. However, it is compounded by the institutional barriers posed by inappropriate, inaccessible language and by lack of access to relevant information.

As well as recognising the importance of word-of-mouth recommendation, and other forms of publicity which do not take literacy or fluency in English for granted, institutions should take steps to ensure that any written publicity actively assists and empowers those who read it. A prominent and positive mission statement in the main community languages, for example, establishes the philosophy of the staff and the institution, and is one way of letting all prospective students know they are welcome.

Similarly, case studies provide positive role models and encouragement that readers can easily identify with. Photographs of particular staff provide a face to go with the name, making it less daunting for people to approach the institution.

Because printed information is loaded with culturally-specific messages and assumptions, it is not enough to rely on a single publicity source, such as a prospectus. Nor is it appropriate simply to translate publicity about particular courses into key community languages. Positive images of black students, user-friendly headings, accessible, relevant information and a prominent commitment to equal opportunities and anti-racism are just as essential.

The realities of diversity and difference within black communities are often subsumed within generalisations and stereotypes. This can be avoided by conducting careful research into local needs, and by targeting specific client groups, for example refugees, Muslim women, refugees who want ESOL (English as a Second or Other Language) for particular purposes, the long-term unemployed or people with special learning needs. This can help to determine both the audience, the kind of information required and the most appropriate form it should take.

Marketing and publicity within the black community goes hand in hand with community consultation, outreach and guidance. Those with responsibilities in these areas should therefore liaise closely and establish procedures to ensure regular and relevant feedback which can influence publicity strategies.

Guidance workers – including those who are not attached to any institution and others whose role involves an element of guidance such as interviewing staff and receptionists – have a key role as mediators. It is they who are responsible on a day to day basis for clarifying information and assisting prospective students to make properly informed choices. A publicity committee or forum should therefore be established to ensure that their views and feedback inform publicity planning.

Marketing and publicity strategies that are genuinely designed to attract people who would not normally use the service should prioritise the use of languages and references that can be clearly understood by everyone – particularly those people who may not be familiar with current educational jargon or the British educational culture from which it stems.

POLYTECHNIC
OF EAST LONDON

Can I talk to someone?

My name is Jasbir Kaur Panesar, I work at the Polytechnic of East London and speak Punjabi. In my work I help Asian women and girls to take up educational courses. I will do my best to answer any of your questions and help you to make the right decision for yourself.

I shall be very happy to talk to you and find out what subject you wish to study and if you need English Language support. I shall also be glad to arrange an appointment to discuss educational opportunities at the Polytechnic of East London and can provide information on courses at local adult and further education colleges and community organisations.

Local courses are run on a part-time and full-time basis. Various courses are run at all levels at Newham Community College, Adult Education Centres and some community organisations. The Polytechnic of East London also offers degree and higher diploma courses in subjects which include Business Studies, Social Sciences, Health Studies, Science, Engineering, Women's Studies, Art and Design, Law, Cultural Studies, Computing, Education Studies, Combined Studies and Independent Study.

I can assist in filling in forms if needed and answer any questions you may have on childcare provision and fees. I can be contacted at:

> Access, Advice and Learning
> Development Unit
> Maryland House
> Manbey Park Road
> London E15 1EY
>
> Tel: 081-590 7722 ext. 4231 or 4254

Educational Opportunities for Asian Women and Girls

Figure 1.7 Extract from Access, Advice and Learning Development Unit, Polytechnic of East London publicity leaflet 1992

Guidelines for Developing More Effective Community Marketing and Publicity Strategies

Know your client groups

☐ Conduct appropriate market research

☐ Develop close links with local black communities

☐ Actively network with other agencies, individuals and non-traditional organisations

☐ Talk to individuals and groups in the community

☐ Promote a service which is seen to be for everyone

Establish your clients' needs

☐ Make full use of available statistics and ethnic monitoring data

☐ Initiate and disseminate research findings which highlight the communities' educational needs

☐ Actively influence colleagues, policy-making and managerial staff to raise awareness of communities' needs

☐ Ensure outreach is permanent, visible and well-resourced

☐ Maintain an Open Door for advice and guidance

Encourage community ownership

☐ Encourage students and local groups to contribute to publicity (e.g. by taking photographs of their activities, contributing their own success stories, etc.)

☐ Encourage students and local groups to participate in competitions to design publicity materials

☐ Encourage students and local groups to distribute leaflets to friends and relatives, local shops, etc.

☐ Use imaginative typesetting, typefaces, colour, graphics and images to assist easy access to information

☐ Use positive, representative images that reflect community diversity, talent and achievement

☐ Publicise local success stories

Be aware of the dangers of marginalisation

☐ Break down barriers through understanding and dialogue

☐ Recognise the importance of word-of-mouth publicity

☐ Use a variety of media to advertise your provision

☐ Find out where people in the community go

☐ Establish a variety of sites for publicity

☐ Translate leaflets and other relevant information into the main identified community languages

☐ Target specific groups and venues for advertising purposes

☐ Request space in shop windows and on notice boards for displays

☐ Ensure that any publicity circulated is up-to-date

Monitor and evaluate your achievements

☐ Encourage students to evaluate marketing and publicity strategies and to suggest improvements or alternatives

☐ Continuously monitor the effectiveness of your marketing and publicity strategies

Don't rely on written publicity

☐ Supplement with
- word-of-mouth
- local and community radio
- regional news
- videos
- canvassing (e.g. in local shopping centre)
- mobile displays
- public talks
- open days
- open evenings
- community festivals

Exploit the community's resources

☐ Use ways of circulating information which are accessible to local communities, such as

- free newspapers
- community newspapers
- ethnic press
- posters and leaflets
- handouts for street distribution
- local exhibitions

☐ Make use of notice boards and displays in

- community centres
- places of worship (e.g. mosques, temples, churches)
- local shop-windows (e.g. halal butchers)
- black bookshops
- shops run by black traders
- housing estates
- launderettes
- doctors' surgeries
- hospitals (e.g. accident and emergency departments)
- libraries
- sports centres
- social services area offices
- housing offices
- Jobcentres and DSS offices
- local schools

Exploit your community networks

☐ Other people have regular access to your potential students. Tap into existing networks established by

- community leaders
- careers and guidance workers
- voluntary workers
- community development workers
- youth workers and social workers
- teachers

☐ Use standard, client-centred headings to organise information. For example:

Why should I choose this particular institution?
(Does it welcome black students; does it take equality of opportunity seriously; does it cater for my particular religious, cultural or linguistic needs; is it for people like me?)

What is available?
(Is the information available in my own language?)

What does this course involve?
(What exactly will I study; does it involve a full-time commitment, or can I attend part-time or on an open learning or flexi-study basis?)

Will I meet the entry requirements?
(Will my overseas qualifications, relevant prior experience, transferrable skills, lack of formal qualifications, standard of spoken or written English be acceptable?)

What will it cost?
(Does it cost as much as I expect it to; where can I get precise information about course fees, loans, grants, etc; am I eligible for assistance from the Access fund or for fee remission?)

Where is it based?
(Is it easily accessible by public transport; is it available at a local or community venue; is there a map and directions?)

When is it?
(Does it fit in with my current childcare, work, domestic or religious commitments; can I join at any time during the year?)

What will be expected of me?
(Will there be coursework; essays; practicals; tests; exams; work experience?)

What support is available?
(What student services can I make use of; will I have access to language and learning support?)

Where will it lead?
(What courses, vocational training, jobs or professional routes are open to me on completing the course; whom do I contact; is there someone I can telephone or speak to; when and where can I reach them?)

Resources

Yearbook of Adult Continuing Education
Published and updated annually by NIACE. Includes comprehensive national lists of press and broadcasting services, directories and journals, post-compulsory providers, TECs, LEAs, etc.

Staff Development for a Multi-cultural Society (particularly Section 2, Unit 4: Marketing and Consultation)
FEU, 1988

Publicity produced by other providers with similar client groups

Useful Contacts

The Voice, 370 Coldharbour Lane, London SW9 8PL. Tel: 071 737 7377

The Asian Times, Hansib Publishing Ltd, 3rd Floor, Tower House, 139-149 Fonthill Rd, London N4 3HF. Tel: 071 281 1191

Local radio presenters and DJs

Local and Community newspapers

Community and Voluntary workers

Organisers of local cultural and religious festivals

Playgroups and Playcentres

Schools and Youthclubs

Advice centres

Educational Guidance providers

Local Careers Service and Jobcentres

EDUCATIONAL GUIDANCE: CASE STUDY

Ms B was 17 years old when she arrived in the UK with her family, which has been waiting over three years for an answer to their asylum application. When she arrived, she had gone into the school system for one year and did one year of an A-level course. However, when she reached 18, the school advised her to transfer over to the local further education college. At first the college was reluctant to accept her onto the second year of A-levels but after the intervention of her teacher, they agreed. Unfortunately, she had to do the A-levels on a part-time basis. As an asylum-seeker, she was liable to pay overseas student fees if she studied full-time in FE. The transfer from school to college also meant that she could do only one of the two A-levels she wanted to do during the day, and she had to go to another local college in the evening to do the second. She obtained her A-levels and wanted to go on to a higher education course to study law. She was endeavouring to get work in a solicitor's office to give her some relevant experience. She applied to the local authority for a grant, having now been in the UK for three years as an asylum-seeker and having therefore satisfied the ordinary residence criterion. However, the LEA refused a grant because, they said, she had not been given an answer by the Home Office about her asylum application.

(Extract from *The Invisible Students*, Section 3: The Need for Educational Advice, World University Service, 1990)

SECTION 2: RECRUITMENT AND SELECTION

2.1 EDUCATIONAL GUIDANCE

The aim of educational guidance is to facilitate access to education and training by identifying and exploring available options. This is best achieved by providing an objective, responsive, client-centred service that operates independently of any institutional imperatives to fill course vacancies.

Effective guidance is not about erecting hurdles or sapping confidence. It is about identifying needs and aspirations, assisting people to make appropriate choices and ensuring that they have all the relevant information they need to set themselves realistic and realisable goals. This is best achieved via informal interviews, where clients are given time to discuss their prior achievements and learning aspirations.

The essential guidance skills of informing, advising, counselling, assessing, enabling, advocacy and feedback each have particular implications when working with black adult learners. Although this does not mean that guidance workers should adopt a special 'kid gloves' approach, which could be experienced as discriminatory or patronising, it does require them to fine-tune these skills by developing the referal networks, information systems, awareness and sensitivity to respond to the specific needs and circumstances of individual black clients.

Advice, for example, cannot be objective where there is a language barrier, or if the interpreter is related to the client or unfamiliar with educational terminology. Likewise, counselling, which is often integral to the guidance process, involves recognising the cultural significance of body language. Assessment may raise particular issues such as the equivalence of overseas qualifications.

An awareness of how racism can undermine confidence and affect relationships with white authority figures is also important, if white guidance workers are to establish a meaningful dialogue with black clients. This is particularly an issue when working with refugees, who may have very recent and traumatic experiences of interrogation or of political persecution based on 'innocent' questions about their education, employment and family history.

The traditional three-term academic year can pose very real difficulties for black adult learners and others whose personal, domestic and financial circumstances require more flexible enrolment options. For providers, the importance of offering all-year guidance – even though enrolment may not be until the following September – cannot be overstated. It should be available and accessible to all prospective students, and should be either a preliminary or integral part of any routine interviewing and assessment procedures for course entry.

To work effectively, staff involved in guidance work must have access to relevant, up-to-date information. This ensures that they can stay abreast of complex legal, social or cultural considerations – particularly those posed by refugees or people on Income Support. There is no substitute for practical experience supported by relevant, on-going training that includes anti-racist guidance strategies, cross-cultural communication, counselling, interviewing and APL skills and regular updating in legal, welfare and educational entitlements. Equally important is a programme of training aimed at interviewing staff, admissions tutors, reception staff, local advice workers and others whose role involves an element of guidance work.

12 Barnsbury Road
ISLINGTON
London N1 0HB
Tel: 01 278 3761/2

EDUCATION ADVICE SERVICE FOR ISLINGTON

GB/NB

13 October, 1988

TO WHOM IT MAY CONCERN

I am writing on behalf of Mr A..... N......, who visited the Education Advice Service on Monday 10th October, 1988.

He expressed concern that he is unable to produce his examination certificates as they have been seized by the police in Iran.

Mr N...... has been resident in this country for 2 years and he has refugee status. While in Iran he graduated in maths and statistics (see enclosed British Council documentation). He completed 1 years' post-graduate study in economics. He has been a maths teacher and has extensive research experience. This was interrupted when he was imprisoned.

When Mr N...... was arrested all his personal belongings were confiscated. Obviously due to the nature of his escape and eventual arrival in this country he is not able to obtain his certificate without putting himself and others at great risk.

I would therefore appeal to you to be sympathetic to these circumstances when considering Mr N......'s application for post-graduate study.

Yours faithfully

ADVISOR

Figure 2.1 Letter from Advisor 'To whom it May Concern'/EASIA (Educational Advice Service for Islington Adults)

EDUCATIONAL GUIDANCE

Issues for Black Adult Learners

- What learning, training and retraining options are available to me? Can I afford them?
- What are the implications for me, my partner and my children?
- Where do I go to get sound advice? Is there a (free?) local or college-based guidance service?
- How formal is the interview? Will it give me the space to discuss my uncertainties, apprehensions, needs, etc?
- Will the advice I receive be up-to-date and impartial?
- Will I understand it?
- Will my (overseas) qualifications and/or previous experience be valued? Will I have to produce any certificates or other evidence?
- Will I have to take any tests? Can I cope with them?

EDUCATIONAL GUIDANCE

Issues for Guidance Practitioners

Do we recognise:

- the need to 'listen to the music behind the words'?
- the need to allow clients to set their own agenda?
- the need to be clear about what the interview can/cannot achieve?
- the need for sensitivity to issues of status, confidentiality, prior persecution?

Do we establish:

- expectations of the interview, course, future prospects?
- prior educational experience or training (how recent)?
- any overseas qualifications (and English equivalency)?
- any current commitments and domestic and family circumstances?
- financial circumstances and motives?
- future plans (e.g. returning to country of origin)?
- current immigration status and any implications for grant entitlement?

Do we explore black clients':

- perceptions, knowledge and expectations of the British education system?
- cultural perceptions of preferred vocational option(s)?
- prior experience?
- language skills?
- literacy and numeracy skills?
- unrecognised, informal and transferrable skills?
- alternative, 'non-traditional' and non-stereotypical options (e.g. alternatives to ESOL, Access)?
- any other written or spoken language(s) and their possible vocational uses?
- 'bridging' options (e.g skills tasters or return to study)?

- flexible, part-time or open learning options?
- voluntary work to gain relevant experience?
- pros and cons of all available options?

EDUCATIONAL GUIDANCE

Issues for Guidance Providers

- Do potential and current students have access to educational guidance throughout the year?
- Have we explored all available funding options such as departmental virement into a centralised guidance budget, partnerships with other providers, TEC funding, etc. to ensure that our guidance provision is properly resourced?
- Do staff involved in guidance have access to a relevant, up-to-date information base?
- Do we allocate sufficient time and appropriate rooms for pre-course guidance work and student interviews?
- Do our guidance staff have access to specialist and bilingual assessors?
- Have we addressed the need for mother-tongue advisors and/or interpreters who reflect the language, cultural values and experience of the black communities we aim to reach?
- Do we provide an ongoing programme of induction and development for staff involved in guidance work?
- Do we discourage the use of unnecessarily formal tests which may assume literacy in English or contain inappropriate cultural bias?
- Does information about our guidance provision reach all sectors of the community?

Our ref BUL/634/8

Your ref

Direct line 071 389 4311

Direct fax

EASIA
12 Barnsbury Road
Islington
London
N1 OHB

The British Council

Promoting cultural, educational
and technical co-operation between
Britain and other countries

10 Spring Gardens
London SW1A 2BN
Telephone 071-930 8466
Telex 8952201 BRICON G
Fax 071-839 6347

13 January 1992

Dear Sir/Madam

Mr F.

Thank you for your letter about the above named.

I should first explain that there is no official equivalence of overseas and British qualifications in Britain. British educational and professional institutions are autonomous and as such reserve the right to make their own decisions on the acceptability and recognition to be accorded to any overseas qualification. We in the National Academic Recognition Information Centre can only pass on information which is based on our experience of the attitudes of these institutions to certain overseas qualifications. Our information should not be treated as an authoritative ruling as to the standard at which the qualifications mentioned below will always be considered in Britain.

With reference to the Ethiopian School Leaving Certificate we advise that this qualification is generally considered comparable to GCSE standard (grades A, B and C) on a subject-for-subject basis when a mark of C or above has been obtained.

The Bulgarian Diploma of Completed Higher Education is a first degree qualification which we advise may generally be considered comparable to British Bachelor (Ordinary) degree standard.

I hope this information is of assistance.

Yours faithfully

Margaret Tudman
National Academic Recognition
Information Centre
Higher Education Department

mt.gmm

Figure 2.2 Letter from the National Academic Recognition Information Centre, British Council

Resources

Educational Guidance with Black Communities: A checklist of good practice
Stella Dadzie, NIACE, 1990

Refugee Education Handbook
World University Service, 1989

International Guide to Qualifications
Mansell

Ethnic Minorities and Careers Services: An investigation into processes of assessment and placement
University of Warwick, 1990

Cultural Aspects of Job-Hunting
Tony Marshall, British Refugee Council, 1989

Careers Guidance with Refugees
Tony Marshall, Refugee Training and Employment Centre, 1992

The Challenge of Change
UDACE, 1986

Useful Contacts

NARIC (National Academic Recognition Information Centre)
c/o British Council, 10 Spring Gardens, London SW1A 2BN.
Tel: 071 930 8466

National Association for Educational Guidance for Adults (NAEGA),
c/o Anne Docherty, 1a Hamilton Rd, Milngavie,
Glasgow G62 7DN

World University Service (WUS), 20 Compton Terrace,
London N1 2UN. Tel: 071 226 6747

2.2 PRE-COURSE ASSESSMENT AND ACCREDITATION

Pre-course assessment should enable adults to demonstrate their level of educational and vocational attainment, while helping the guidance worker or tutor to identify their individual learning needs and progression options. It should involve the identification and, where appropriate, accreditation of any prior experience or learning (APEL) to assist when planning and negotiating entry to their chosen course.

APEL is, by definition, a complex and time-consuming process. In addition to establishing the nature and equivalent value of any formal qualifications, it involves a detailed exploration of the individual's personal and employment history, including any skills acquired from working in the home, raising children, organising household budgets, doing voluntary work, or pursuing hobbies and specialist interests.

Where existing skills are largely informal, APEL workshops or modules can provide invaluable support to students when preparing for course entry or exit, by assisting with the development of personal portfolios or records of achievement. These provide examples, evidence and testimonials that demonstrate the individual's skills and level of academic and vocational competence. For black students, they are a highly effective means with which to challenge the racist assumptions and low expectations of prospective course tutors and employers.

It is important to make the assessment process as unthreatening as possible, particularly for black adult learners and others who may be unfamiliar with APEL or the cultural and academic requirements of formal assessment. Staff responsible should avoid interrogative or intrusive questioning, and be prepared to explain the purpose and process of APEL as well as any assessment criteria and other requirements. They should also be able to 'tease out' and recognise transferrable skills, establish the equivalence of overseas qualifications, and be sympathetic to the special circumstances of refugees and asylum-seekers, who may be unable to produce certificates and other formal evidence.

Encouraging students to evaluate their own prior learning and achievements is the most effective way of gaining initial insight into their background, particularly where their education was acquired overseas. Self-assessment – if necessary with the assistance of an interpreter – can also help students to identify relevant experience and any language or learning support needs they may have. Apart from providing a better understanding of the student's abilities, potential and learning options, this client-centred approach is more likely to encourage an early sense of direction and positive achievement, particularly in black adults whose confidence may have been sapped by past experiences of racism.

Sensitivity to the many factors which may inhibit black adults undergoing assessment and APEL can be heightened by means of training for all staff involved in the formal or informal assessment of potential students, including guidance, admissions and interviewing tutors.

A relevant training programme would aim to develop good interviewing skills and highlight the dangers of stereotyping, cultural and linguistic bias, or mistaking lack of confidence or limited communication skills for lack of intelligence. It would also aim to raise awareness of the many existing barriers to fair assessment faced by black adult learners.

Where students do not meet the required standards, providing sympathetic feedback enables them to identify the skills and knowledge they need to acquire. A detailed record of the assessment, including any marked scripts or assessor's comments, can be a great help when preparing for future assessments or negotiating entry to alternative provision.

Barriers to Fair Assessment

☐ Black adults are likely to have had fewer opportunities for work experience, employment or professional practice in this country due to employers' racism.

☐ Refugees and others who trained overseas may not be familiar with specialist language, British legal frameworks and technical terms.

☐ The standards and concepts used in vocational assessment may be culturally biased or assume an unspecified level of competence in written or spoken English.

☐ Some black adults may need access to an interpreter, a dictionary or other forms of English language support when being assessed.

☐ Black adults are more likely to be disadvantaged if the assessor has no experience of working with linguistic or cultural minorities.

☐ Assessors and professional bodies are often unfamiliar with education and training systems in other countries and reluctant to acknowledge equivalence.

PRE-COURSE ASSESSMENT AND APEL

Issues for Black Adult Learners

- Do I know what assessment and APEL involves?
- How do I go about getting my previous (overseas) qualifications and prior experience accredited?
- Can I cope with tests?
- Will my performance suffer because of nerves or lack of confidence?
- Will my performance suffer because of the attitudes, approach or cultural assumptions of the assessor?
- Is my written and/or spoken English up to the task? (What is expected of me?)
- Can I ask for an interpreter; a dictionary or some other form of language support?
- What happens if I 'fail'? (What other options are available to me?)

PRE-COURSE ASSESSMENT AND APEL

Issues for Staff Involved in Pre-course Interviews and Assessment

- Do our pre-course assessment and APEL methods empower students to make choices based on clear information about their options and abilities?
- Are they designed to promote access to appropriate learning or assessment programmes?
- Do we provide pre-course skills tasters; portfolio-building workshops; and/or APEL modules?
- Do initial interviews offer students guidance and counselling to identify needs, abilities and aspirations, prior to any pre-course assessment requirement?
- Are pre-course assessment and APEL fully integrated into our centralised admissions procedures?
- Do we offer continuous assessment on all vocational and academic learning programmes?
- Have we developed a range of pre-course assessment and APEL resources, including:
  - clear information for students about assessment, accreditation and APEL criteria
  - verbal, written or self-assessment exercises that review and assess prior learning
  - initial diagnostic assessments
  - assessment for career direction
  - assessment for language aptitude
  - criteria for credit transfer and accumulation
  - work experience placements offering on-the-job assessment
  - learning contracts
  - action plans
  - records of achievement

- Do we have access to a relevant database that includes:
    - details of other agencies' APEL and accreditation criteria
    - details of local, national and in-house learning options
    - information about alternative progression routes
    - information about fees, costs, grants, student loans

Resources

Refugee Education Handbook
World University Service, 1989

International Guide to Qualifications
Mansell

Survey of Numbers of Black Adults with Professional Qualifications Gained Overseas
Stella Dadzie, NIACE, 1993

Useful Contacts

NARIC (National Academic Recognition Information Centre)
c/o British Council, 10 Spring Gardens, London SW1A 2BN. Tel: 071 930 8466

National Association for Educational Guidance for Adults (NAEGA), c/o Anne Docherty, 1a Hamilton Rd, Milngavie, Glasgow G62 7DN

National Council for Vocational Qualifications, 222 Euston Rd, London NW1 2BZ. Tel: 071 387 9898

World University Service (WUS), 20 Compton Terrace, London N1 2UN. Tel: 071 226 6747

Local Open College Networks

Regional Access Federations

2.3 RECRUITMENT, SELECTION AND ADMISSIONS

Recruitment, selection and admissions procedures can be frustrating for any student, however familiar she or he may be with the requirements of the system. For black adults, who may have already encountered a series of hurdles *en route*, the interview or enrolment experience could prove a genuine – and perhaps final – disincentive.

With the trend towards amalgamation and the consequent growth of large, multi-sited institutions, students face an increasingly complex and bewildering experience. Higher education institutions, already hamstrung by impersonal PCAS and UCCA procedures, are likewise faced with the challenge of 'humanising' their admissions process in an effort to increase adult access. An all-year admissions unit, or a centralised system operating across a number of access points, can minimise frustration and bureaucracy to the advantage of everyone, particularly black adult learners and others who find large institutions daunting.

Admissions procedures need to be rational, user-friendly and responsive to the full range of potential applicants. Although procedures may vary according to the nature and level of the course and the requirements of sponsors and validating bodies, wherever possible they should involve individual guidance and selection interviews and efficient referral systems giving potential students access to financial advice, language support, APEL and specialist assessment.

Staff involved in interviewing and assessment need access to an up-to-date, centralised database, showing course vacancies, entry criteria and other relevant information. How well-informed they are will depend largely on efficient channels of communication. If tutors have set recruitment targets for particular courses, admissions staff will need to know this. Similarly, if tutors are to identify under-represented groups, they need access to relevant ethnic and gender data collected at the point of admission.

Because of growing pressure to improve student retention and examination performance, institutional gatekeepers may be tempted to see their role as keeping 'problem' students out. This is clearly incompatible with their guidance function, which should be about enabling and empowering individuals as they negotiate their way into and through the institution. Application forms and admissions interviews should include space to identify prior learning and experience, so that languages spoken, child-rearing experiences, voluntary work, overseas qualifications and any other relevant skills can be properly identified and accredited.

For black adults, there are likely to be any number of institutional barriers to negotiate prior to or at the point of entry. Staff involved in interviewing and pre-course assessment need to be aware of such issues, and competent to address them in a student-centred way. In addition to other training implications, this requires a sound knowledge of students' legal, welfare and financial entitlements and – above all – adequate time and privacy.

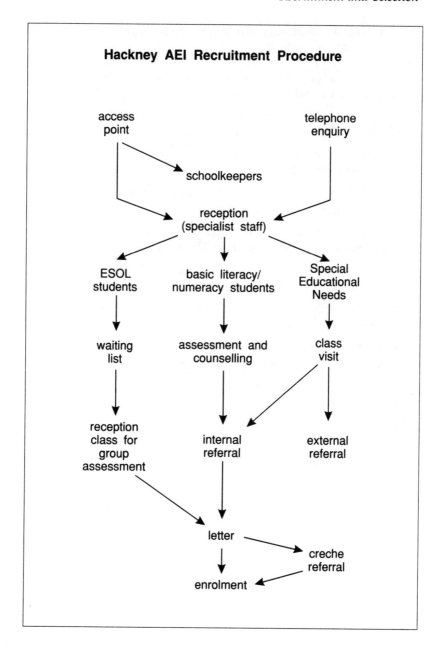

Figure 2.3 Centralised Admissions Procedure, Hackney AEI, 1992

Barriers to Recruitment for Black Adult Learners

☐ Fees or grant eligibility requirements which may debar them from certain full-time options.

☐ Temporary residence, immigration or refugee status which affects their grant or fees entitlements.

☐ Unnecessary entry requirements such as (British) GCSEs or formal, culturally-biased tests.

☐ Failure of the institution to recognise and accredit equivalent overseas qualifications.

☐ Lack of appropriate or adequate ESOL support, particularly assistance with technical and academic terminology.

☐ Lack of relevant work experience or sponsorship due to the racism of employers.

☐ Lack of confidence in formal education, due to negative prior experiences in school.

☐ Lack of confidence when dealing with mainly white organisations or white authority figures.

☐ Lack of familiarity with Britain's educational system and learning culture.

RECRUITMENT, SELECTION AND ADMISSIONS
Issues for Black Adult Learners

- What are my skills? Are they relevant?
- Which skills do I want to develop? Why?
- Do I have any relevant qualifications?
- Can they be accredited?
- Is my English up to it?
- Can I cope with tests?
- What demands will be made on me? Will they conflict with my cultural, religious, domestic or childcare commitments?
- How much is this going to cost? Am I eligible for any financial support or fee remission?
- How am I going to support myself, my family and my children? What are my entitlements?
- Will becoming a student cause problems with the DSS or the Home Office, for example? What support is available?

RECRUITMENT, SELECTION AND ADMISSIONS

Issues for Practitioners

- How do we ensure that interviews enable students to validate their own prior learning and achievement?
- When we identify students' language and learning support needs, is our provision flexible enough to offer them an appropriate individual learning agenda?
- Do we ensure that reception, guidance and interviewing staff have a clear understanding of the aims, method, content and outcomes of our course?
- Do our interviews allow time to explore the costs, potential difficulties and personal implications for each student?
- How efficient are our internal and external referral systems?
- Do we accept and accredit overseas qualifications and/or transferrable skills?
- Do we offer appropriate pre- and on-course language support for overseas students, refugees and speakers of other languages?
- Do we give helpful feedback to unsuccessful applicants?

RECRUITMENT, SELECTION AND ADMISSIONS

Issues for Managers

- Do we operate an efficient centralised admissions service?
- Do we allocate sufficient time and adequate accommodation to interviewing and admissions staff?
- Have we established appropriate guidance and referral systems?
- How could our in-house communications be improved to ensure that admissions and teaching staff are properly informed?
- Do we have a policy of recognising and accrediting overseas qualifications?
- Do we ensure that interviewing and reception staff have access to relevant training?
- Have we established clear criteria on the fees chargeable to overseas students, refugees, asylum-seekers and people on income support?
- Do we have a fair and equitable system of fees subsidy? Are students made aware of how to apply to the Access fund?

Resources

Racism and Recruitment
R. Jenkins, Cambridge University Press, 1986

Admissions, A New Beginning
Video and training pack, NCVQ and Wirral Metropolitan College, 1989

Adults Welcome: A checklist for colleges
REPLAN, 1988

Access to FE for Black Adults
FEU REPLAN

Useful Contacts

Educational Grants Advisory Service, c/o Family Welfare Association, 501–503 Kingsland Rd, London E8 4AU

2.4 STAFFING ISSUES

Staff Appointments

Institutions that are staffed by an all-white workforce or confine black staff to temporary, non-managerial or servicing roles give potential and incoming black students a clear message that public declarations about black access and equality should not be taken too seriously.

Attempts to recruit black students should therefore go hand in hand with a declared anti-racist staff recruitment policy, designed to attract and encourage black appointments at all levels within the organisation. This ensures that the institution reflects the communities it serves, and gives students access to the advice, support and expertise of black/bilingual staff as they adjust to the demands of adult learning.

An anti-racist staff recruitment policy should include a commitment to:

- promoting the benefits of cultural and linguistic diversity within a workforce that is representative of the communities served
- appointing black staff at all levels, including managerial and decision-making posts
- making support for equal opportunities policies a condition of service for all staff
- conducting ethnic monitoring and regular review of all applications and staff appointments
- providing explicit job specifications for all posts
- recognising the prior learning, relevant experience or overseas qualifications of applicants
- placing advertisements in the ethnic/community press and with other relevant community agencies
- agreeing standard (open) questions for all candidates
- applying objective weightings to desired or demonstrable competences
- ensuring a representative interviewing panel in terms of both race and gender

- implementing democratic short-listing and decision-making procedures for all appointments

Where black applicants do not come forward in sufficient numbers, despite these endeavours, other, longer-term strategies may need to be considered, such as:

- the use of targeted publicity to raise awareness of employment (teaching or support staff) opportunities for black and ethnic minority adults
- the promotion of teacher training opportunities such as City & Guilds 730, Access to BEd or courses for overseas qualified teachers
- open days and short taster courses offering guidance and jobsearch skills to would-be black tutors.

These initiatives have the dual purpose of creating a pool of potential black tutors and encouraging black access to full and part-time teaching opportunities in the wider community.

Staff Development

The confidence of black staff, once in post, can be easily undermined if colleagues are resentful or unclear about the criteria and rationale for their recruitment.

Black students face similar difficulties where tutors lack the skills and confidence to implement the institution's anti-racist policy and meet their particular learning needs.

Managers therefore have a responsibility to ensure that all staff have access to an on-going programme of staff development providing, among other things, an opportunity to discuss the arguments for positive action, the targeting of under-represented groups, and other key aspects of the institution's anti-racist policy.

Staff training will prove a more effective long-term investment if delivered in line with a staff development policy requiring all training to be backed up by:

- adequate human and material resources
- a needs analysis of staff at all levels, including managers, governors and those responsible for security, reception, canteen and caretaking services

- incentives such as accreditation or time off in lieu to encourage maximum attendance
- an analysis of local learning needs
- positive aims and outcomes designed to encourage change
- practical strategies with a focus on action-planning
- regular review and evaluation to ensure that the policy and training remains relevant
- induction, appraisal, training and on-going support for all staff, including part-timers
- targeted events for black staff to provide a forum for networking and the development of managerial and other relevant skills.

TO ALL BLACK STUDENTS IN FURTHER EDUCATION, HIGHER EDUCATION, COMMUNITY COLLEGES, COMMUNITY CENTRES AND PROJECTS.

We are very pleased that you are continuing your own education and would like to put a proposition to you.

At some stage, either while you are a student or when you have completed your course, would you consider becoming a Part-Time Adult Tutor?

We would like to invite you to an informal Open Evening on Tuesday 10th March, 7.30-9.30pm at The Moat Centre, Melbourne Road, Highfields, Leicester in order to show you what is involved in being a part-time adult tutor and how you might apply for a post.

If you are interested and want to find out more, please complete the reply slip and return it to Sue Houlton, Community Education Office, 15 New Street, Leicester.

"Each one, Teach one"

✂ -

REPLY SLIP

I am interested in finding out about being a

I will attend the informal Open Evening at t
Tuesday 10th March 1992

NAME: . . . .

ADDRESS: . . . .

TEL. NO: . . . .

Please return to Sue Houlton, Comm

WANTED!

Black part-time adult tutors

Have you ever thought you might like to be a part-time adult tutor, but do not know enough about it? Now is your chance to find out!

Come along to our open evening and we will tell you:-
- what is involved in being a part-time tutor
- how to apply for a post
- about training opportunities

It's on Tuesday 10th March 7.00-9.30
At the Moat Centre, Melbourne Road, Leicester
Light refreshments will be served

LEICESTERSHIRE COUNTY COUNCIL

Figure 2.4 Recruiting black teaching staff: Leicestershire County Council flyers

TEACHING INFORMATION DAY FOR OVERSEAS QUALIFIED TEACHERS

HAVE YOU BEEN A TEACHER IN YOUR COUNTRY?

DO YOU HAVE QUALIFICATIONS FROM YOUR COUNTRY?

Do you think that you could, and would, like to be a teacher here?

We want to support YOU

NEWHAM COMMUNITY COLLEGE

Come to
The Barclay Hall Centre
Green Street, London E7 8JQ
Wednesday 16th January 1991, 9.30am

TASC TEACHING AS A CAREER

to find out the ways you can pursue your ambition of becoming a teacher.

Please book your place by telephoning 081-472 2785,
or writing to the address below, before 3rd January 1991

Bharti Ruwala
170 Harold Road Centre, London E13 0SE

Creche facilities are available, but please book early

Figure 2.4 (continued) TASC publicity - Newham Community College

STAFF RECRUITMENT AND DEVELOPMENT

Issues for Black Staff

- Does my own experience and that of other black colleagues suggest that equal opportunities and anti-racist principles are applied to staff appointments and promotions?
- What kind of support is available to me? Does it include:
  - adequate induction?
  - a clear job description?
  - regular staff development and training opportunities?
  - mentoring from another black staff member?
  - work-shadowing to gain insight into managerial roles?
  - a support group for black staff?
  - regular appraisal?
  - appropriate managerial support?
- How can I avoid isolation? What black staff and/or community networks exist in this institution, local area or region?
- Is my cultural or linguistic expertise valued? What (voluntary) forums exist for me to contribute to:
  - student support, advice work, counselling?
  - community liaison?
  - course reviews?
  - staff awareness of cultural and anti-racist issues?
  - policy development?
  - decision-making?
- How can I avoid professional ghettoisation? Could my original subject specialism suffer as a result of my race equality role or activities?
- What grievance procedures exist should I need to complain about the racism of students, colleagues or managers? What could inhibit me from using them?

STAFF RECRUITMENT AND DEVELOPMENT
Issues for Managers

- Do we appoint black staff and governors to ensure proper representation of the communities we serve at all levels?
- Do we avoid concentrating black staff in temporary, part-time posts by ensuring that they have access to mainstream appointments?
- Do we value the particular cultural or linguistic expertise of black staff by encouraging their contribution to all areas of the service?
- Do we provide black staff with targeted training and relevant support to deal with institutional racism; feelings of isolation and/or tokenism; the risks of professional ghettoisation?
- Do we expect black staff to contribute specialist skills (e.g. interpreting, counselling, community outreach) without formal managerial acknowledgement?
- Do we encourage understanding of anti-racist policy among both staff and students by encouraging widespread discussion, consultation and 'ownership'?
- Do we encourage white staff to participate in regular anti-racist training?

Resources

Staff Development for a Multi-Cultural Society
FEU, 1988 (A comprehensive training resource providing practical information, checklists, training exercises, etc. for colleges.)

Useful Contacts

Stella Dadzie
Front Line Training
149 Albert Rd
London N22 4AQ
Tel: 081 881 0435 (For training on all aspects of black adult learning covered in this book, and a range of other areas.)

AIMER (Access to Information on Multicultural Educational Resources)
Faculty of Education and Community Studies
University of Reading
Bulmershe Court
Earley
Reading RG6 1HY
Tel: 0734 3218810 (For database of information on multicultural and anti-racist resources and a postal enquiry service.)

Local TEC (Training and Enterprise Council)
(For details and directory of local training organisations offering anti-racist and equal opportunities training.)

Further Education Unit
Citadel Place
Tinworth Street
London SE11 5EH
Tel: 071 962 1280

Staff College
Coombe Lodge
Blagdon
Bristol BS18 6RG
Tel: 0761 462503

2.5 ETHNIC MONITORING

Monitoring can help an institution to identify areas where black students are over- or under-represented, and to respond more flexibly to the social, cultural and learning needs of its clients. It involves requesting essential information at the point of enrolment, supplementing it with more detailed data, and applying that information systematically to the planning and quality review of all courses, services and policies.

Because questions about ethnic and national identity may be regarded as intrusive, ethnic monitoring should be an anonymous, confidential and, where possible, voluntary exercise. For the benefit of the many people, both black and white, who regard it with some suspicion, the anticipated benefits of the exercise need to be carefully outlined. To perform this role, personal tutors, reception and admissions staff need training so that they can feel confident to explain the purpose of monitoring and clarify the different categories involved. Written guidelines should also be available to students, where necessary translated into the main community languages.

Monitoring at the point of enrolment is most effective when the results are centralised, computerised and combined with other relevant data within the existing management information system. An ethnic breakdown of students' progression, examination results and drop-out rates, for example, can provide invaluable insight into the success or otherwise of an institution's declared commitment to its black students.

In the long term, however, monitoring should aim to establish not only the overall percentage of black clients who 'succeed' in formal terms, but also the numbers requiring childcare facilities, cultural and dietary considerations, wheelchair access, ESOL provision and other forms of learning support. This is best achieved by means of student surveys, questionnaires, tutorial discussions and regular marketing exercises which actively involve students in identifying and articulating their own needs.

The collection and dissemination of data in a clear, accessible form is vital if course teams and providers of other services are to take proper account of the practical implications for marketing, planning and quality review purposes. This is increasingly important, given the growing reliance of colleges on external contractors to provide catering, security and other essential services.

All too often ethnic monitoring is regarded as an end in itself, or conducted as a paper exercise to satisfy the Education Department or particular funding bodies. Frequently, the ethnic categories specified by such bodies are ambiguous or fail to take account of the complexity and diversity of the different black communities served. A strict adherence to the ethnic monitoring requirements of external bodies is therefore unlikely to result in useable data.

Given the range and complexity of potential needs, including those of women, linguistic minorities, refugees and others in the black community, it is no longer sufficient to know that a percentage of students on a given course have identified themselves as 'Asian'. A Vietnamese refugee, for example, will probably have very different cultural and learning needs from a Ugandan Asian, yet it is likely that, in the absence of any alternative categories, both would tick this box.

Consequently, if ethnic monitoring is to be an effective means of counteracting institutional racism in the form of under-representation, marginalisation and vocational ghettoisation, providers need to identify both the national and ethnic origins of potential and existing clients. Above all, they should develop an on-going dialogue with local black communities, with a view to supplementing and interpreting the resulting data in a creative, non-stereotypical way.

STUDENT QUESTIONNAIRE

This questionnaire provides you with an opportunity to think back over the time you have spent at Haringey College so far and to make any suggestions or criticisms of the course you are on or the College as a whole.

It is designed to establish whether you are satisfied with:

* The system of enrolment and induction
* The general advice and information you've been given
* The support, counselling and educational guidance services
* The teaching and learning resources available to you
* The organisation of your course

Your tutor will probably ask you to complete the questionnaire during your tutorial and will take your responses back to the course team, who will discuss them and try to take account of your group's views when they are planning and running the course next year.

Please consider each question seriously before selecting or writing down your answers. Try to make sure that what you say genuinely reflects your own experience and opinions. You are not required to give your name and since answers will be confidential, you may be as open and honest with us as you like.

Your views should help us to identify any changes that may be needed to improve the service we offer. We will consider your views carefully wherever resources and practical arrangements permit.

Despite the recent cuts in the college's budget, we aim to meet the needs of every student to the very best of our ability. With your help we will come closer to achieving this.

Figure 2.5 Extract from Student Survey, Haringey College

E.3   WHEN YOU CONSIDER YOUR EXPERIENCES BOTH INSIDE AND OUTSIDE THE CLASSROOM HOW SUCCESSFUL DO YOU THINK THE COLLEGE HAS BEEN IN PUTTING INTO PRACTICE:

* ITS POLICY AGAINST RACISM AND DISCRIMINATION?

VERY SUCCESSFUL   QUITE SUCCESSFUL   UNSUCCESSFUL

COMMENTS ....
....
....
....

* ITS POLICY TO CATER FOR THE DIFFERENT CULTURAL AND
LANGUAGE NEEDS OF STUDENTS?

VERY SUCCESSFUL   QUITE SUCCESSFUL   UNSUCCESSFUL

COMMENTS ....
....
....
....

* ITS POLICY TO PROMOTE EQUAL OPPORTUNITIES
FOR WOMEN STUDENTS?

VERY SUCCESSFUL   QUITE SUCCESSFUL   UNSUCCESSFUL

COMMENTS ....
....
....
....

E.4   DO YOU HAVE ANY SUGGESTIONS ON HOW WE COULD IMPROVE RELATIONS BETWEEN STUDENTS AT THE COLLEGE?

                              YES   NO

COMMENTS ....
....
....
....

Figure 2.5 Extract from Student Survey, Haringey College (continued)

ETHNIC MONITORING

Issues for Black Adult Learners

- Why does everyone keep asking me the same questions?
- Is this just another form-filling exercise?
- Do I have a choice?
- What happens if I don't supply the information?
- How would I describe myself?
- Which box am I expected to tick?
- Is it clear what I am being asked for (e.g. nationality; colour; ethnicity; religion)?
- What do they want this information for?
- Who wants it anyway?
- Who else will have access to it?
- Is there any chance that my personal details could end up being given to someone else (e.g. the police; social security; Home Office; racist organisations)?
- How will it benefit me if I provide this information?
- How will it benefit others in my community?
- Is there any evidence that this information is being acted upon?

ETHNIC MONITORING

Issues for Staff and Managers

- What human and material resources are available to carry out this work?
- How efficient is our existing management information system?
- Are the ethnic categories we use adequate? Do they tell us what we need to know?
- Are the ethnic categories we use ambiguous? Is it clear whether we are asking for nationality, ethnicity or colour?
- What other data should we be gathering? How can we ensure that information is cross-referenced?
- How can we ensure that staff and students are properly briefed on the purpose and anticipated outcomes of ethnic monitoring?
- What other ways are there to gather or supplement this information?
- Have we explored the advantages and disadvantages of using:
  - student reviews?
  - targeted questionnaires?
  - one-off marketing exercises?
  - student surveys?
  - headcounts?
  - tutor-led appraisals?
  - discussions in tutorials?
  - other ways of gathering data?
- Do the data reach those who need it such as course planners; staff responsible for marketing and publicity; interviewing and admissions staff, etc.?

- Do they know what to do with the data?
- In what ways are staff actively encouraged to respond to any under-representation, ghettoisation, low achievement, high drop-out, poor progression rates, etc.?
- How do we ensure that other agencies have access to the relevant data?
- Do we include ethnic monitoring data in our annual reports; quality reviews; general publicity; other public documents?
- Do we feed information back to those on our networks, including independent guidance services, local TEC, local schools, other local agencies?

Resources

Ethnic Monitoring in Further and Higher Education
FEU

Staff Development for a Multi-Cultural Society (Book 2, Unit 2: Ethnic Monitoring)
FEU, 1988

Useful Contacts

Commission for Racial Equality

Local Community Relations Council

Local Race Equality Unit

Local community groups

SECTION 3:   ON-COURSE

3.1 ETHOS AND ENVIRONMENT

An appropriate ethos and environment for black adult learners is one which reflects an active commitment to anti-racism, cultural pluralism and access. This requires institutions to respect and encourage the diversity of cultures represented in the student body and the wider community; and to provide services, facilities and learning contexts that are tailored to these.

An institution which publicly declares its commitment to anti-racism yet fails to reflect this commitment in the make-up of its staff, the content and delivery of its curriculum and the nature of its extra-curricular provision cannot expect to be taken seriously. It should be the responsibility of all staff to ensure that students can learn in an environment that does not ignore, undermine or assault their sense of who they are.

To this end, black staff, students and local communities are an invaluable – and often overlooked – resource. Their particular skills – such as the ability to speak certain community languages, to provide mother-tongue advice, demonstrate traditional handicrafts or perform traditional music or poetry – should be valued and encouraged. They should also be supported in their efforts to effect institutional change and invited to contribute to those decisions and activities which determine the institution's character and ethos. Positive, non-Eurocentric images – in publicity, newsletters, teaching resources and on noticeboards – can also help to reinforce this ethos of community ownership.

The appointment of black staff at every level within the teaching and support hierarchy will both enrich the institution and provide black students with positive role models. Positive or targeted action may be needed to redress staffing imbalances, particularly at managerial levels, where black staff are frequently under-represented.

As well as helping to pinpoint areas of under-representation, the collection and dissemination of ethnic data, often regarded as a necessary bureaucratic ritual to meet Department for Education or sponsors' funding requirements, is essential if staff are to identify students' religious, dietary, cultural and social requirements. The results should inform the planning and delivery of every aspect of the service, from the food on offer in the canteen to the decision-making processes which determine the institution's overall mission.

Busy Zahida could be a winner

"I'm busy but I enjoy myself."

There's no doubting either. Zahida Khan is one of Newham's nominees to the Outstanding Adult Learners' Award, and she's come through many hurdles to be at the threshold of her final goal.

Zahida has only been an adult learner for five years. But in that time she has taken no fewer than six adult courses and is now on a seventh – the Licensed Teachers course at the Polytechnic of East London, which will qualify her as a secondary school teacher.

Zahida had the benefit of a good-quality university education in her native Pakistan. Soon after she came to Britain twenty years ago, she was the proud mother of two daughters, although the younger was to be severely disabled. As her children grew up, she wanted to prove that her earlier education was still useful – even though the British government wouldn't accept her qualifications for teaching purposes.

"I started off with some volunteer teaching at Sarah Bonnell School, helping parents learn English." says Zahida. *"Then I took my first adult course, a certificate for teaching English to adults."*

Tutor Bharti Ruwala nominated Zahida for the Award. *"She has dedicated her life to improving her personal qualities so that she can become a competent professional – in a country where everything is different from how she was brought up"* says Bharti. *"Her studies have made her more confident and skilful."*

Zahida agrees, particularly that she has gained in self-confidence. But demands have been considerable – she can start with prayer at six in the morning, through household tasks and studies in the day, to teaching in the evening and written work until 2 am.

"Maybe I enjoy teaching more than learning" says Zahida. *"I want to encourage my students into further study, especially women – I tell them Yes, it's good, look at me!"*

Figure 3.1 Extract from Newham Community College newsletter

Community News

UNIVERSITY TO EXPLORE LINKS WITH COMMUNITY

computer link up first step towards breaking down the traditional 'ivory tower'

Talks have already taken place between representatives of the Centre for the Study of Public Order (Leicester University) and members of Leicestershire's African Caribbean community, concerning the strengthening of links between the University of Leicester and the local community.

of Public Order is looking into linking the university's massive mainframe computer with the Raddle Training Centre on Berners Street. It is hoped that with this link up, members of the local African Caribbean community will have access to the University's computing facilities, thus further enhancing Raddle's training programme.

Direct Effect

As a direct effect of the research, serious discussion has taken place involving the university, the African Caribbean Support Group and the Raddle Training Centre, concerning bridging the gap between the community and the traditional 'ivory tower' University environment. As a first stage in the process of bringing the community and the university together, The Centre for the Study

Training

Also under consideration is the possibility of the university acting as a satellite for Raddle and training members of the African Caribbean community for the university's certificate in Information Technology. It is hoped that around twelve African Caribbean people will benefit annually from the training programme.

'African Caribbean People in Leicestershire' Research Project   Five

Figure 3.2 Extract from African-Caribbean Newsletter, Leicester

Actions which are clearly hurtful to others include:
1. Physical assault against a person or group because of colour or ethnicity.
2. Derogatory name-calling, insults and racist jokes.
3. Racist graffiti or any other written insult.
4. Provocative behaviour such as wearing racist badges or insignia.
5. Bringing racist material such as leaflets, comics or magazines into the college.
6. Making threats against a person or group because of colour or ethnicity.
7. Racist comment in the course of discussion or conversation in college.
8. Attempts to recruit staff and students to racist organisations and groups.

These actions are unacceptable anywhere. The college will tackle them on four fronts:

(a) deal with the perpetrator

(b) aid and support the sufferer or sufferers

(c) establish the line of responsibility

(d) deal with the impact of the incident upon the college.

HARASSMENT

(a) The college will have clearly defined procedures for dealing with complaints of harassment and will ensure that members of staff and students are aware of these procedures.

   i) Members of staff, accompanied by a friend if they wish, should <u>normally</u> take their complaint to their Head of Department, who will initiate the appropriate action. Staff must be prepared to put their complaint in writing if required. If there is difficulty in following this agreed procedure, the complaint should be taken to the Vice-Principal.

   ii) Members of staff may also take their complaint to the appropriate union or staff association.

   iii) Students should take their complaint to their course tutor, a student counsellor or another member of staff whom they trust. They may if they wish be accompanied by a friend. The complaint should than be put in writing and taken to the Head of Department concerned, who will initiate the appropriate action.

   iv) Students will be advised that they may seek Student Union support if they so wish.

   v) All cases of harassment should be recorded by the Head of Department concerned and a record kept in the Vice-Principal's office, to which the Equal Opportunities Co-ordinator(s) will have access.

(b) Members of staff and students must feel supported when making their complaint.

(c) Actions which constitute harassment are defined in the Appendix.

Figure 3.3 Extract from City and East London College Anti-Racist Statement, 1988

ETHOS AND ENVIRONMENT

Issues for Black Adult Learners

Is my ethnic, cultural and or religious identity reflected in:

- **positive images**
  e.g. in publicity, displays, the content of the curriculum and the ethnic make-up of staff?
- **support services**
  e.g. access to mother-tongue advice and counselling?
- **the food available in the canteen**
  e.g. vegetarian or ital dishes, halal meat, etc.?
- **acknowledged religions**
  e.g. allocated prayer room, time off for religious observances and festivals, staff sensitivity to the effects of fasting during Ramadan?
- **women-only provision**
  e.g. allocated common-room space, single-sex sport and leisure activities, classes catering for Muslim women?
- **regulations concerning dress**
  e.g. the wearing of tams, turbans, religious jewellery or traditional clothing?
- **celebrations of cultural diversity**
  e.g. in displays and exhibitions, public entertainment, dance, music, art?

ETHOS AND ENVIRONMENT
Issues for Staff and Managers

- Do our security arrangements discourage community access?
- What procedures exist to ensure that ethnic monitoring data inform the planning, delivery and quality review of all our services?
- What consultation and evaluation procedures are in place to ensure that students and local communities can influence the planning, provision and review of student services and facilities?
- Do we encourage parents and community groups to contribute to the development and delivery of extra-curricular activities? What learning opportunities do we offer them?
- Do we make full use of the resources in local communities such as bilingualism, specialist knowledge and formal and informal support structures? Are relevant skills accredited?
- Do we ensure that learning resources contain positive, non-stereotypical images?
- Have we developed positive action strategies to address the under-representation of black staff and students and encourage black access?

Resources

Staff Development for a Multi-Cultural Society (Booklet 2, Unit 7: Ethos and Environment)
FEU, 1988

Useful Contacts

Afro-Caribbean Education Resource Centre (ACER), Wyvil Rd, London SW8 2TJ. Tel: 071 627 2662
(ACER develops and advises on learning materials; also has books, videos and posters for sale and an extensive reference library.)

Other providers with a clientele similar to your own, for advice and ideas

Students' Union representatives

Local community groups

Local or Regional Multi-cultural Resource Centre

3.2 PERSONAL SUPPORT

Like all students, black adult learners do not leave their personal 'baggage' at the door of the institution. They bring with them the same range of concerns about family and personal relationships, childcare, money, crime, sexuality, health and housing as their white counterparts. However, because of institutional racism and their particular cultural context, these concerns – along with the insecurities they may feel about returning to study – may be exacerbated or require more complex solutions.

The establishment of an effective tutorial system, allowing each student to receive peer group support from other students on the course as well as individual support from their personal tutor, is essential if the effects of such issues are to be minimised. This is especially important for part-time, evening and open learning students who are more likely to be isolated; and for students following modular courses (such as GCSE or Dip. HE) where individualised learning programmes may inhibit the development of a discrete group identity.

Regular group tutorials can help students to contextualise their personal circumstances and share the inevitable insecurities experienced by those who are not used to the rigours of studying. If structured around a coherent tutorial programme of comprehensive and extended induction, on-going self-evaluation, current health, welfare and social issues, visits and social activities, course review and evaluation, vocational guidance and progression planning, they can be an ideal forum for personal and group development, and a highly rewarding learning experience for both the students and the tutor.

Tutors are most effective when they are sufficiently motivated to get to know each of their students individually. They also require a clear definition of their tutoring role and responsibilities, and access to relevant resources and training. Basic counselling skills, for example, cannot be taken for granted, particularly cross-cultural counselling, which is a prerequisite if tutors are genuinely to assist black students. This includes knowledge of when and how to refer students whose language, personal problems, immigration status or cultural context may require specialist help from external agencies.

Good tutoring practice aims to support and encourage each student to take full advantage and control of their learning opportunity. A 'sink or swim' or *laissez-faire* approach cannot, by definition, address personal and group issues of racism and diversity. Ideally, therefore, tutorial provision should be regular, compulsory and include space for both groupwork and individual sessions. For this, tutors need access to a private room where they can see individual students in confidence; a classroom or base for group sessions; and a timetable which takes account of the *real* time involved in offering quality tutorial support.

Tutors should also be encouraged to contribute to building up a centralised bank of tutorial resources which are relevant to all students and readily accessible.

Black students in all- or mainly white institutions, and those who are concentrated on low-level, Access, ESOL or outreach provision, may feel ignored or isolated. As mediators between the institution and its clients, tutors have a responsibility to keep their students informed of developments, events and activities which address their social, cultural and educational needs. To this end, effective communications systems are essential. A regular weekly or fortnightly tutorial bulletin, containing relevant information, notices and announcements and a review of student activities and achievements, facilitates cross-institutional communication with students, while at the same time helping to promote a positive ethos and encouraging students to identify with the institution as a whole.

Mentoring schemes which actively involve members of the community in the lives and aspirations of students, have proved a particularly effective form of personal support for black students. Such schemes have grown from the recognition that institutional racism frequently deprives black people of positive role models. The mentor, typically someone who has 'achieved' in their own profession, provides advice, motivation and a friendly ear, as well as opportunities to clarify career goals through work-shadowing and the sharing of personal and professional experiences. Like many other areas of provision, the success of mentoring schemes depends largely on the commitment of both the tutor and the institution to developing and sustaining genuine community partnerships.

"A MENTOR"

By Vik Bhandari

Many Black students have the ability to do well and succeed in life, yet they lack the motivation to achieve their aspirations and goals. What chance have they got at having a decent, respectable job, when their parents and friends before them had so many difficulties and barriers to overcome?

The North London College Mentor Project is a way to break this mode of thinking! Students are given the confidence to believe in themselves and strive to perform to the best of their abilities. In a world today where with the right frame of mind 'barriers' are easily overcome, second best is not good enough.

Mentors have a vital role to play in the project. Not only do they provide support to the student, they are a valuable role model. A budding accountant would benefit from having a professional accountant as their mentor. With regular meetings, arranged in informal surroundings, the student has the opportunity to express her/his uncertainties in their life and receive guidance on matters relating to accountancy, both as a study subject and as a profession, and also advise on general, and sometimes personal matters.

Over the duration of the academic year, it is hoped that a successful student/mentor relationship extends much further than the formal requirements of the project and be-comes one which is of a more personal and friendly nature. Through this the student should feel free to contact the mentor for advice outside of the arranged monthly meetings. Equally, the mentor can widen the student's horizons by exposing them to the social functions and events which they might otherwise not have the opportunity to attend or experience.

Being a mentor is very rewarding. One feels that through your own experiences and mistakes they have helped, guided and made an impact on a student, who could become one of tomorrow's leaders.

Working in Law

Melanie De Freitas

I have found the Mentor Project enjoyable and helpful. All the students who decided to join this project have gained many things, such as work experience, confidence building and self-assertion.

As I wish to continue my career within Law, this project has provided me with the chance to get involved with a solicitors firm called Stennett and Stennett. Mr M. Stennett, my mentor, has given me a chance to see how a law firm operates. This has been made possible for me because I joined the Mentor Project.

Figure 3.4 Extract from North London College Mentor Programme 1989-90

Resources for Personal Tutors

☐ Induction resources or handbook containing:
- map and site plans
- timetables
- term dates
- who's who on the staff
- information about available services, facilities, the Students' Union, extra-curricular activities, etc.
- information about available learning support
- information about available financial support (e.g. Access or hardship fund, grants for books, tools or equipment, travel subsidies, etc.)
- outline of equal opportunities and anti-racist policies
- copy of student code of conduct
- copy of student contract
- clarification of what constitutes racial or sexual harassment
- details of grievance and disciplinary procedures
- health and safety guidelines

☐ Information, advice and general resources, including:
- welfare rights, jobsearch skills, vocational options
- topic sheets and videos covering social issues such as racism, aids and drug-abuse
- updated referral lists of agencies offering specialist help and advice
- regular bulletins containing cross-college memoranda and information about social and community events
- standard letters about course requirements, non-attendance, etc.
- funds for visiting speakers, social outings and visits to industry or receiving institutions
- guidelines for work experience placements
- guidance materials and input from guidance staff about students' progression options
- jobsearch activities, including interview preparation and application skills
- standard application forms (e.g. UCCA, PCAS)

- pro forma for assessment, accreditation and profiling
- course evaluation and review questionnaires
- procedures and forms for recording achievement and monitoring student progression
- procedures and forms for maintaining centralised student records

PERSONAL SUPPORT

Issues for Black Adult Learners

- During induction:
  - Where is everything?
  - Who is everybody?
  - How will my religious, dietary and cultural needs be met?
  - Can I cope with this course?
  - What language and learning support is available?
  - Should I be doing something else? If so, what, and whom do I ask for advice?
  - How do I get out of here?

- On the course:
  - How am I getting on?
  - Why do we have to do?
  - Am I getting what I wanted from this course?
  - Do I need additional support (e.g. ESOL, study skills)?
  - Does this course reflect my own needs, aspirations, life experience and cultural expectations?
  - How am I to deal with the pressures of coursework, examinations, peers, family and childcare?
  - Who can I talk to about these and other personal pressures?
  - Have I been treated fairly? What do I do if I want to make a complaint?

- During transition and progression:
  - What have I gained from this course?
  - What do I want to do next?
  - What do I need to do about it?
  - What will be required of me?
  - What kind of language, financial or childcare support will be available?

Issues for Personal Tutors

- During induction:
  - Do I have access to appropriate resources for student induction?
  - What resources and strategies are available to help me to form the group and establish group identity?
  - What is the best way to familiarise students with relevant policies and procedures?
  - Am I confident to handle issues which may arise during discussions of the anti-racist policy? What training is available to me?
  - How well are individual students adapting to this learning environment? Does anyone need additional help or referral?

- During the course:
  - How well have I established a rapport with individual students?
  - Do I have the necessary tutoring skills to meet individual students' needs? What training is available to me?
  - What resources and strategies will help me to foster students' self-confidence and positive self-awareness? Are there people in the local communities who could act as mentors or positive role models?
  - How do I ensure that students are able to take responsibility for their own learning and take advantage of available learning resources?
  - Does the behaviour, timekeeping or performance of any student indicate that s/he needs more personal support, counselling or referral to other agencies?
  - Am I able to respond quickly to warning signals such as lateness, non-attendance, poor performance, etc? How effective are procedures for liaising with subject tutors or other staff involved?
  - Do I have the time, skills and resources to help students review and reflect on their individual progress?

THE PERSONAL TUTOR'S JOB DESCRIPTION

STUDENT INDUCTION
Meeting with new students; introducing them to the course, the College and its facilities, their subject tutors and each other; assessing their needs and goals.

HOLDING REGULAR TUTORIALS
Organising regular group and individual tutorials; reviewing students' personal objectives and individual progress; instigating discussion of relevant personal/social/educational issues.

GIVING SUPPORT TO STUDENTS
Offering support to individual students, particularly those experiencing personal, financial, domestic or study difficulties; referring students to appropriate services or outside agencies, where appropriate.

CIRCULATING RELEVANT INFORMATION
Disseminating relevant information; informing colleagues on the course team of any issues which might hinder their ability to teach the group or individual students effectively.

KEEPING RECORDS/PREPARING REFERENCES
Managing all records of students' progress and attendance; ensuring that adequate information is available for the preparation of references and profiles.

ASSESSMENT
Encouraging regular self-assessment; constructing personal profiles for continuous/final assessment; gathering and collating the views of colleagues on students' individual progress; conveying such views to the students, when appropriate.

PLACEMENTS
Ensuring that suitable work experience/training placements are found which reflect individual interests and aspirations; offering support to students while on placements in the form of visits, briefing, debriefing and, where necessary, intervention.

PROGRESSION
Reviewing individual progress; discussing future plans; ensuring that students are aware and able to respond to any requirements from the receiving institution/employer.

COMPLAINTS
Acting as a mediator between staff and individual students when complaints are made; representing students in disciplinary hearings or course team discussions; ensuring that any complaints, whether by staff or students, are responded to.

Figure 3.5 Personal Tutor's Job Description, Haringey College

- Are students receiving sufficient educational and vocational guidance?

• During transition and progression:
  - What forms of assessment and evaluation are available to help students evaluate their achievement?
  - Has each student had an opportunity to explore the range of progression options available to them, and their respective implications?
  - Have I ensured that references, profiles and appropriate personal and academic records are available for each student, future employers, future course tutors or my successor?
  - Have we met our contract and course aims? How could we improve this provision?

Behaviours that do not Promote Equality

Taken from 'Under New Management' – LGTB. (Publications) 1990

Being patronising: making condescending remarks, for example using words like 'dear' or statements like 'Well of course we all know how to ... don't we?'

Stereotyping: putting people into categories on the basis that they are all alike in certain respects, for example, expecting all disabled people to be in wheelchairs, using 'he' to refer to managers.

Discounting: not taking into account what a person has said or contributed, for example a black person says something but it is ignored: when a white person makes a similar statement it is taken on by the group.

Using 'put downs': for example, 'You know you are useless at figures, so why don't you use the calculator and do it properly?' This sort of behaviour reinforces a person's lack of confidence and self esteem, and belittles their efforts.

Discriminating: treating the person differently (often less favourably) to others in the same circumstances. For example, 'Part of the reason why we didn't suggest you for this project is because we didn't see how you could put the time into it and look after your children at the same time'. As a result of this you may be underestimating the person's capabilities and limiting available options and opportunities.

Taking a 'colour-blind approach': not recognising that the person in front of you is black and that this is an important feature of the person's make-up and existence, and part of what makes her or him an individual.

Making prejudiced remarks: making direct or indirect negative references to a person's race, sex, age, based on ignorance or stereotypes, for example, 'It's nothing to do with you being black'.

Colluding: taking the side of, or making excuses for the person or group being prejudiced or discriminating, for example, 'He didn't mean to be offensive, you know what men are like, it's the way they are brought up'.

Making racist and sexist remarks: for example remarks that on deeper inspection show that you hold the attitude that women and black people are inferior to you.

We aim to respect equally all learners and users regardless of age, gender, ethnic origin or previous educational attainment – and to encourage such respect between learners.

Figure 3.6 Extract from Induction and Support Pack for Part-time Tutors of Adults, Leicestershire Community Education Service

PERSONAL SUPPORT
Issues for Managers

- Do all courses offer appropriate tutorial support, including distance or open learning, part-time and evening courses?
- Are all tutors familiar with the responsibilities of their role? What arrangements are in place to ensure that new and existing tutors are given appropriate induction, training and support?
- How can we ensure that personal tutors' timetables reflect the real time involved in tutoring?
- Have we considered the use of private study periods, reading days, staggered lunchbreaks, distance learning methods, etc. to accommodate an on-going rota of regular, individual tutorials?
- What administrative support is available to assist tutors in their efforts to retain and motivate students? Does it include a typing service; centralised records, etc.?
- Have we prioritised the development of a tutors' handbook, a student induction pack and centralised tutorial resources?
- Are there any staff whose temperament, attitudes or beliefs make them unsuitable as personal tutors?

Resources

Tutoring
FEU, 1982

How Responsive is Your College to the Needs of Unemployed Black Adults?
NIACE REPLAN, 1988

The Heart of the Race: Black women's lives in Britain
B.Bryan, S.Dadzie and S.Scafe, Virago, 1982

Just Lately I Realise: Stories from West Indian lives
Gatehouse, 1985

Finding a Voice: Asian women's lives in Britain
Amrit Wilson, Virago, 1978

Breaking the Silence: Writing by Asian women
Centreprise, 1984

A Place to Stay: Memories of pensioners from many lands
Pam Schweizer (ed.), Age Exchange, 1984

Our Lives Series, including:
From East to West, Linh Hoa
So Many Things I Could Have Written, Asha Mohammed
From Sound to Silence, Rashida Abedi
Standing on My Own Two Feet, Faizia Zaman
Croydon English Language Scheme, 1992

Useful Contacts

The Mentor Programme, North London College, 444 Camden Rd, London N7 0SP. Tel: 071 609 9981

The Mentor Programme, South Manchester College, Fielden Park Centre, Barlow Moor Road, West Didsbury, Manchester M20 8PQ. Tel: 061 434 4821

Mature Students' Union, 6 Salisbury Rd, Harrow, Middlesex HA1 1NY. Tel: 081 863 3675

3.3 CURRICULUM ISSUES

An anti-racist curriculum is one which incorporates the history, contributions and perspectives of black peoples into every aspect of its content and delivery. Black issues and viewpoints are seen as integral rather than as a topic to be bolted on to an essentially Eurocentric syllabus. Students are actively encouraged to question the negative language, stereotypes and assumptions associated with blackness, and to value the role which black and other non-European peoples have played in the development of the communities, societies and world in which we co-exist.

A multi-cultural curriculum, on the other hand, endeavours to foster respect for other cultures by promoting an appreciation of cultural relativity. Its emphasis is typically on issues of cultural difference and diversity, rather than on the social-economic, historical and political connotations of the subject under discussion. This can lead to the representation of black people and cultures as 'curious' or 'exotic'. As a consequence, students may fail to make the connection between racism and culture, while those who are white may continue to see the world through Eurocentric eyes.

Some subjects – for example, history, literature, art or environmental studies – appear to lend themselves more readily to an anti-racist curriculum. The relevant research is easier to locate, and debates about black people's contributions and concerns in these fields have to some extent been publicly aired. However, there is no subject area which can justify ignoring the role, influence, achievements and philosophies of non-European societies in its history and development. Nor is there a single area of the curriculum which does not lend itself to anti-racism.

Because of the emphasis on multi-cultural *content* rather than anti-racist *strategy* in recent years, teaching staff may be less likely to appreciate this fact. They may therefore fail make the links between the language and references they use, the teaching styles they adopt, and the ways racism is perpetuated. This is especially true of teachers of apparently 'neutral' subjects such as maths, typing, engineering, business studies and other subject areas where socio-political, cultural or anti-racist issues do not seem immediately appropriate to meeting course objectives. There are, however, a number of relevant teaching strategies which can be adopted, ranging from modifying the syllabus so that it becomes more student-centred, to challenging traditional ways of interacting with students in the classroom.

Despite valid arguments about the specialist nature of individual courses or the restrictive requirements of validating bodies, it is the attitudes of teachers themselves which pose the greatest barrier to anti-racism in the curriculum. Most staff can be encouraged to develop the necessary level of awareness and a familiarity with the range of teaching strategies and resources available to them, if relevant guidelines and on-going training are provided.

Collaborative curriculum development projects, workshops and course team discussions which encourage teaching staff to focus not simply on content but also on their classroom organisation, styles of delivery and communication skills, have proved the most effective way of addressing such needs. As an interim measure, staff may also choose to trade classes, allowing those who have relevant knowledge to input into courses or subject areas where anti-racist expertise is lacking.

The promotion of public or cross-institutional events such as lectures, talks, plays or filmshows which highlight anti-racist issues can also play an important role in raising the profile of anti-racism among staff and students.

The development of an anti-racist curriculum should not, however, be limited to discussions about content and teaching styles. In the interests of all adult learners, staff should adopt a holistic approach to course and curriculum planning, taking account of the timing, cost and mode of delivery; the need for integral language, learning and childcare support; and the provision of a quality system of tutoring and student support.

Anti-racist Teaching and Learning Strategies

☐ Make a mutual contract with students which specifies acceptable classroom behaviour for both students and tutor in the context of the equal opportunities/anti-racist policy.

☐ Negotiate and adhere to clear groundrules which encourage a classroom ethos of mutual respect, equal value and learning from shared experience.

☐ Be prepared to explain and, where necessary, justify student-centred methods – particularly to students who are used to more directive, didactic or traditional methods.

☐ Conduct a group skills audit as a way of demonstrating the value of each individual's prior learning and experience, including languages spoken and cultural expertise.

☐ Identify and build on issues which are relevant to students' lives as an initial vehicle for learning.

☐ Use early tutorials and group discussions to explore students' prior learning experiences and identify any individual anxieties, perceptions and expectations.

☐ Encourage mutual support and understanding by highlighting common experiences and concerns.

☐ Ensure that learning aims and outcomes are clearly stated, both for the overall course and each individual session.

☐ Begin with confidence-building exercises and be prepared to give praise and individual attention to adults who have been out of education for some time.

☐ Encourage participative seating arrangements, including circular seating, paired activities and small group work to promote good group interaction and cross-cultural communication between black and white students.

☐ Adopt student-centred approaches to teaching and learning, building on life experiences and using students' prior learning and cultural perspectives as a starting point and on-going focus.

☐ Organise tasks and activities in a way that encourages students from different ethnic backgrounds to interact and learn from each other.

101

☐ Use a variety of learning methods, including experiential tasks, group discussions, collaborative project work, student reviews and regular self-evaluation.

☐ Use a variety of teaching styles to maintain an appropriate balance between theory, experimentation, intuitive learning and observation.

☐ Pay attention to language and delivery – strong regional accents, talking too fast, using unnecessary jargon or providing culturally-exclusive examples.

☐ Be conscious of the way language can perpetuate racist assumptions (e.g. black-white/civilised-primitive/superior-inferior connotations).

☐ Give clear aims, messages and written or verbal instructions.

☐ Use regular summaries and student feedback to check understanding of key learning points – particularly of bilingual students.

☐ Pay attention to the learning environment – positive images in posters and displays, absence of noise and distractions, planning for 'creature comforts', etc .

☐ Avoid public reprimands and put-downs; treat adults as adults and equals.

☐ Encourage student autonomy by building confidence and promoting independent learning.

Devising a Course

When first thinking about your course, think about the historical and contemporary contribution that Black people have made to the subject, and the contribution black cultures across the world are currently making to it.

Some of the courses we teach have a direct connection to the phenomenon of racism:

- include in the course the 'Black' history of the subject;
- encourage students to question the absence of a Black dimension, Black experience or point of view;
- trace modern day connections between Britain and the two/third's world;
- enable students to see the subject from non-European perspectives;
- search out for yourself materials about your subject which incorporate a Black perspective, and which are written by Black people;
- ask your Head of Department for material, teaching ideas and views on course design.

In Lesson Planning

- Devise strategies so that all class members can contribute.
- Make sure White students do not dominate discussion or get all your attention.
- Listen to Black students' contributions and value them.
- Include Black students in groups, making sure they are not on the edge or always at the back during a demonstration.
- Accept that racism is a daily experience of Black people's lives and may well be part of a contribution to the class.
- Ditch the myth that racism is a 'chip on the shoulder' – it isn't!
- Make it your responsibility to challenge any unnecessarily negative remarks about Black people – particularly broad generalisations which group all Black people together.
- Don't assume or imply that the western experience of civilisation and 'development' are superior – remember what Gandhi said when asked what he thought about western civilisation: 'It would be a good thing.'

Figure 3.7 Extract from Learning in Black and White. One of a set of leaflets from Wandsworth Adult College

Language

A lot of our language uses Black to mean bad or negative e.g. blackmail, black spot, black patch etc. White, on the other hand mostly carries connotations of goodness, purity etc. This tends to perpetuate the stereotype that Black – including Black people – is negative. TRY and use alternative expressions.

Our classrooms and our teaching materials speak a language too:
- make sure pictures have positive images of White AND Black people;
- make sure the Black images are POSITIVE and break the well-worn images of Black people as singers or footballers, doing menial tasks, or looking helpless and starving.
- use strong, assertive pictures, for example of Black women doing technical tasks, or Black men caring for children.

Culture

Bring into your teaching connections with other cultures – particularly Black cultures. Making these cultural connections broadens out the curriculum and enriches your subject. But, do be careful. It has pitfalls too:

If you use examples from another culture:
- make sure that you give the example a proper context;
- make sure you do not inadvertently turn it into something 'exotic';
- make sure you use contemporary examples as well as historical ones;
- make sure you invite any students from that culture to talk about it – but don't expect them to be the 'expert' – it's not fair.

However, anti-racism is best served by helping students see the political, social and historical connections between the Black and White world, not the cultural differences.

Figure 3.7 (continued)

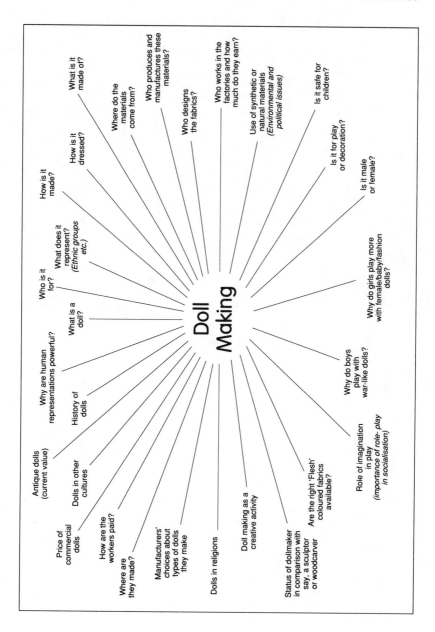

Figure 3.8 Anti-racist approaches to the curriculum
(Wandsworth Adult College)

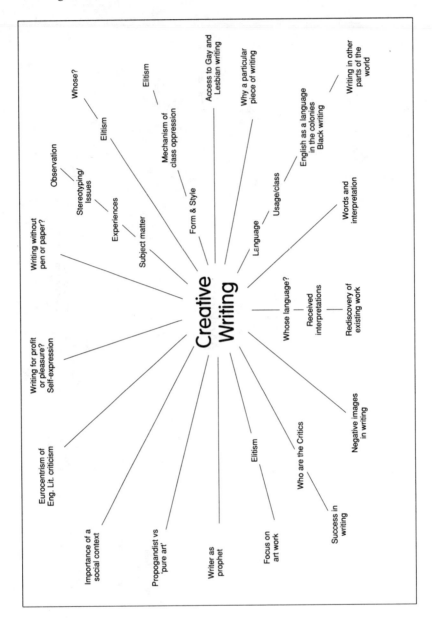

Figure 3.8 (continued)

Anti-racist Curriculum Strategies

☐ Modify teaching materials so that the people and contexts referred to reflect social and ethnic diversity (e.g. Ms Patel instead of Mr Smith).

☐ Challenge racist stereotypes in text-books, teaching materials, training videos, etc. (e.g. black people confined to menial, non-managerial roles).

☐ Question and replace materials which ignore, diminish or criminalise black people.

☐ Acknowledge the positive contributions, inventions, discoveries and achievements of black people associated with your subject area.

☐ Demonstrate black achievement in areas other than sport and music.

☐ Use visual aids which include positive images of black people in assertive, non-stereotypical roles.

☐ Encourage students to consider the experiences and perspectives of non-European cultures.

☐ Challenge inequalities and social injustice – both in the curriculum and the classroom.

☐ Recognise and question the effects of racism by omission.

☐ Challenge negative remarks and generalisations about black people.

☐ Be conscious of the need to give equal attention to black students.

☐ Encourage black students to contribute their knowledge and experience of their own history and culture.

☐ Value and encourage bilingualism.

CURRICULUM ISSUES

Issues for Black Adult Learners

- Does this course acknowledge me, my culture, language and history?
- Does it marginalise, stereotype, ignore or negate my experience in any way?
- Do the tutors appear to respect, encourage and value my input?
- Do tutors encourage black and overseas students to contribute information about the cultures, philosophies, laws, social or vocational attitudes in their countries of origin?
- Do the tutors give respect and equal attention to all students?
- Does the course provide adequate space and time for me to evaluate my achievements and progress?
- Does the course offer me the language support I need?
- Do I have access to learning support classes or workshops where I can improve my study skills, literacy and numeracy, computing and IT skills, jobsearch and interview skills, etc.?
- Is help available for the purchase of essential textbooks and special equipment?
- Are students encouraged to contribute to course evaluation and planning, and to other relevant decision-making processes?

CURRICULUM ISSUES

Issues for Practitioners

- Do we include the promotion of anti-racism as one of our key learning outcomes?
- Do we stereotype or prejudge students' capabilities on the basis of their linguistic, social or economic needs?
- Do we share and evaluate classroom teaching strategies designed to promote an ethos of equality?
- Do we have an understanding of the way language can offend and marginalise black students?
- To what extent does our curriculum reflect the diverse cultures of our students, local communities and society?
- What curriculum planning and development mechanisms are in place to ensure that the content, language and teaching strategies are relevant to all students?
- Do we vet textbooks and learning resources for racist innuendos and Eurocentric bias?
- Do we challenge and discourage racist assumptions in textbooks, teaching media, student discussions, etc.?
- Do we regularly update our materials to take account of technological, social and global changes?
- Do we ensure that students have access to integral language and learning support, relevant to the full range of abilities?

CURRICULUM ISSUES

Issues for Managers

- What resources have we identified to support this area of work?
- Do we have a whole-institution approach to curriculum planning?
- Is the development of an anti-racist curriculum fundamental to our concept of quality assurance?
- Do we provide regular and on-going staff development to support and encourage anti-racist curriculum and teaching strategies?
- Do our staff appraisal procedures include an evaluation of lecturers' anti-racist teaching skills?
- Are our assessors and curriculum managers trained to detect and challenge racist content and practice in the classroom?

Resources

Assessing and Evaluating the Curriculum for Unemployed Black Adults
FEU, 1990

Curriculum Development for a Multi-Cultural Society
FEU, 1985

Mainstream Curricula in a Multi-Cultural Society
FEU NAME, 1989

Staff Development for a Multi-Cultural Society (Booklet 3, Curriculum Change; Booklet 4, Examples of Curriculum Development)
FEU, 1988

Anti-Racist Science Teaching
Dawn Gill and Les Levidow, Free Association Books, 1987

Developing Language Awareness. Materials for Business Studies Courses
FE Business Studies Group, 1992

Language Awareness in Business Studies. Assignments and Materials Developed in 1986-87
Brixton and Hammersmith College, 1992, available from Language and Literacy Unit, Southwark College

'Language, Learning and Race', Margaret Robson, *Developing Communications Skills for a Multicultural Society*
FEU, 1987

Useful Contacts

Afro-Caribbean Education Resource Centre (ACER), Wyvil Rd, London SW8 2TJ. Tel: 071-627-2662
(ACER develops and advises on learning materials; also has books, videos and posters for sale and an extensive reference library.)

AIMER (Access to Information on Multicultural Educational Resources), Faculty of Education and Community Studies, University of Reading, Bulmershe Court, Earley, Reading RG6 1HY. Tel: 0734 3218810
(For database of information on multi-cultural and anti-racist resources and a postal enquiry service.)

Institute of Race Relations, 2–4 Leeke Street, London WC1X 9HS.
Tel: 071 837 0041
(For advice, information and access to comprehensive research library.)

3.4 ON-COURSE ASSESSMENT

On-course assessment should be part of a process that provides students with an on-going means of establishing and recording their progress, and objective evidence of their end-of-course achievement. As such, it should be both formative and summative, taking place before, during and towards the end of the learning opportunity.

A traditional view of student assessment regards unseen written tests as the only valid yardstick for measuring progress. This overlooks the considerable benefits to the student of regular self-evaluation against known criteria when producing coursework or setting personal targets; and the value of regular tutorials, in which students can review their progress with the help of a sympathetic tutor.

To this end, tutors should aim to demystify the assessment process, so that students can have greater control of their own learning. Adult learners, particularly if unfamiliar with the learning culture in this country, need to be given clear assessment criteria. They should receive clear information about the requirements of continuous assessment, as well as guidelines for decoding the grades, abbreviations and clichés used by tutors when marking course and examination work.

Where formal tests and examinations are necessary, these need to be screened for any mono-cultural references or linguistic bias which might place black students at a disadvantage. Wherever possible, culturally biased assessment can be replaced or supplemented by other more flexible assessment methods, designed to establish the student's competence and understanding, as well as formal knowledge.

Alternative methods might include:

- mother-tongue assessment
- practical on-the-job assignments
- simulated workplace assignments
- personal portfolios
- written or verbal self-evaluation exercises

- informal one-to-one interviews or tutorials
- individual or peer group reviews.

Where assessment criteria are determined by external bodies, tutors can play an important role in raising the awareness of external moderators and assessors of the needs and concerns of black students. This is best achieved in partnership with relevant black community organisations, employers, professional bodies and individual black specialists, who are an often-overlooked resource. As well as advising lead bodies when training standards are developed, they may be prepared to participate in the piloting of work-place assessment schemes, the support and mentoring of individual students or the provision of much-needed work experience.

The maintenance of up-to-date, centralised records of assessment and progression ensures that students can have access to accurate personal references once they or the tutor have left the institution. This is especially important for the long-term unemployed, women who have worked in the home, refugees and others with no alternative referees.

OVERALL CRITERIA FOR GRADING

A – 70% and above   DISTINCTION
An outstanding answer that presents an interesting question. Demonstrates knowledge and understanding of concepts and debates and ability to think critically about links with practice and experience. Well structured arguments and use of relevant evidence and imaginative sources including making links with equalities issues. Ability to be self-reflective. Imaginative presentation and use of appropriate format.

B – 60-69%   MERIT
A sound answer in approach and content with evidence of reading and some awareness of approaches/perspectives. Well organised overall and interesting to read with clear understanding of equalities perspectives. Analysis and evaluation have been attempted and links between concepts and experience and self-reflection developed. Sources and evidence are adequate but could be developed further to extend overall level of argument and debate. Planning and presentation good..

C – 50-59%   CREDIT
An answer which gives fair coverage to the question or topic but may be too descriptive or generalised and needs focus. Some presentation of material and evidence of thinking for self. May be gaps in argument and critical use of evidence and uneven use of equalities perspectives. Needs work on links between concepts and analysis of practice/experience which are uncertain and limited. Could improve ability to be self-reflective. Planning and presentation may need some work in parts.

D – 40-49%   PASS
Some attempt to answer question and use of experience, material and sources, but may be used inappropriately and uncritically. Too descriptive and needs to develop understanding of concepts. Evidence of gaining skills but needs to develop ability to analyse experience and self-reflection. Sources and equalities perspectives could be addressed more thoughtfully in relation to topic. Planning and presentation need work to aid overall work.

E – 39% and below   FAIL/REFERRAL (borderline)
Answer relies on minimal range of detail or simply repetition. May consist of string of weak assertions/opinions which may not relate to each other and which lack evidence. Needs more attention to ability to develop skills of self-reflection. More practice on focus, structure and planning. Only slight awareness of equalities perspectives.

F   Very weak fail
Little understanding of question/topics, poorly organised, muddled and use of irrelevant material described incorrectly. Little evidence of analysis, planning or skills development.

Figure 3.9 Criteria for Grading – Department of Extra-Mural Studies, Birkbeck College (Certificate in Urban Community Studies, 1992)

STUDENT SELF EVALUATION SHEET

Please complete this cover sheet and attach it to each piece of course work

NAME OF COURSE   ....

NAME OF STUDENT   ....

NAME OF TUTOR   ....

DATE submitted to tutor   .... DATE returned   ....

TITLE OF COURSE WORK   ....

   ....

A

Check the following:-

Presentation (is it easy to read and clear?)

Spelling

Sentence construction (if you read it aloud does it make sense?)

Argument (does it follow through logically?)

Is there a question in the title?

References (are they correctly listed?)

Bibliography

B

Now answer the following:-

1. What are you pleased with in this piece of work?

2. In what ways (if any) have you improved?

3. What would you do differently in future?

4. Identify any gaps in your knowledge you would have liked to explore.

Figure 3.9 (continued) Student Self-evaluation Sheet

On-course Assessment

Issues to Raise with Assessors

☐ How flexible is the route to assessment and qualification in our particular professional or vocational area?

☐ Are the entry criteria explicit?

☐ Do the guidelines for professional or vocational recruitment discourage racial, cultural and linguistic discrimination?

☐ Is the number of successful and unsuccessful black applicants monitored, to determine whether these guidelines are effective?

☐ Are overseas equivalent qualifications recognised and accredited?

☐ How fair are existing methods of assessment? Are they culturally or linguistically biased?

☐ Do they include any unnecessary culturally-specific jargon, references or terminology? What assistance can be given to students whose first language is not English?

☐ Are any black professional groups, community organisations or individual black specialists involved in the development and piloting of standards for vocational qualification?

☐ Are bilingual and multi-lingual assessors recruited who can contribute to assessment teams and offer mother-tongue support to those with limited English?

☐ Is the use of self-assessment and informal assessment methods encouraged, wherever appropriate?

☐ Do our networks include black professional bodies and individuals, both in Britain and overseas?

☐ Do we specify relevant or equivalent experience rather than rigid routes to qualification for accreditation purposes?

☐ Do we accept voluntary work, work-place simulation, work in the home, childcare and employment training as evidence of competence or prior experience?

☐ Do we promote flexi-study, open and distance learning options for APEL purposes?

☐ Do we monitor the recruitment, progress and outcomes of black students for planning and review purposes?

☐ Do we have access to suitable training in the assessment and accreditation of black adult learners?

Resources

Cultural and Linguistic Bias in Assessment. A project report
Harminder Bisla, FEU, 1992

Useful Contact

National Council for Vocational Qualifications, 222 Euston Rd,
London NW1 2BZ. Tel: 071 387 9898

3.5 LANGUAGE SUPPORT

Effective English as a Second or Other Language (ESOL) provision facilitates students' access to the full range of available education and training options. It caters for a diversity of personal, social, linguistic and vocational needs, both general and specialist, and requires tutors to take proper account of individual motivation and rates of progression. Where appropriate it aims to make people literate in their own spoken language as a means of achieving literacy in English.

Tutors frequently assume that those who lack English communication skills must be illiterate, uneducated or unskilled. This tendency to equate language competence with literacy affects established second and third generation communities as well as refugees, many of whom are highly qualified and multi-lingual. Because of the diversity of language needs represented within black communities, ESOL provision needs to be flexible and wide-ranging, and should not be confined merely to 'bolt-on' classes. The assumption that all prospective students of ESOL require either basic English language survival skills or Cambridge Proficiency is narrow and outmoded.

The initial assessment of a student's language competences is a vital part of the pre-course guidance and APEL process. To ensure that students of ESOL do not find themselves trapped on low-level courses offering no formal accreditation or continuity, their learning contracts should always specify individual progression options. These are best identified during a process of quality – and where appropriate mother-tongue – guidance. Any advice should include information about available language support, and be mapped so that ESOL learners have access to viable routes into employment and further learning opportunities.

Assessment for course entry should be closely related to the language demands and expectations of their preferred mainstream course. This can only occur if the language skills necessary for the successful completion of the course – and modules within it – are clear and negotiated at the outset. Courses catering for ESOL learners should therefore be carefully planned to ensure that any language requirements are explicit and reflected in the teaching methods and entry criteria. Flexibility and certification are central to the development of any meaningful language policy. Institutions should aim to offer dynamic entry and exit points, including modularised courses, credit accumulation, flexible and open learning options, and differing levels of specialist and non-specialist provision. Language tuition should be complementary and wherever possible integral to the student's chosen course of study. This requires close liaison and collaboration between ESOL and subject tutors in the planning, delivery and assessment of student assignments.

Bilingual and multi-lingual tutors are a potentially invaluable human resource in this area, both as ESOL and subject specialists. Their importance to students as role models is likely to be complemented by cross-cultural communication skills, high levels of commitment and a sensitivity to students' cultural needs and attitudes. Appropriate induction, support and training are, however, essential for such staff if institutions are to benefit fully from their skills and expertise.

Managers need to be aware of the dangers of professional ghettoisation, especially where the majority of black staff are ESOL appointments dependent on short-term funding.

LANGUAGE SUPPORT

Issues for Black Adult Learners

- How will available ESOL provision meet my particular language needs as well as my personal, vocational or professional goals?
- Will it lead or contribute to a recognised qualification?
- Have the language demands of each element of the course(s) I've chosen been made clear to me?
- Is the content, method and style of teaching appropriate to my skills and circumstances, my degree of language competence, my prior qualifications?
- Do the language support classes complement the course I am studying? Will they help me to meet the specific language requirements of written assignments, etc.?
- Do the lecturers appear to value my bilingual skills and my other skills and knowledge?
- Am I encouraged to contribute or explain things in English or in my mother-tongue, if appropriate?
- Do I have continued access to mother-tongue guidance, assessment and tuition, if I need it?

- Do ESOL, guidance and subject tutors participate in a regular, collaborative forum in order to plan and develop the language curriculum?
- Have we identified the language skills and competences required for the successful completion of each course?
- Have we modularised each course into manageable units of language learning and competence?
- Are these made explicit to students, guidance and interviewing staff, language support tutors, assessors?
- Do we make bilingualism and language awareness a starting point for classroom learning and teaching?
- Do we prepare students for informal or experiential teaching styles and student-centred approaches?
- Do we try to establish what students already know, and use this as a basis for further language learning?
- Have we modified teaching resources and assignments so that relevant information is presented in a clear or tabular form and excludes unnecessary details or jargon?
- Do we explain the value of credits and the purpose of different forms of assessment?

LANGUAGE SUPPORT

Issues for Managers

- What resources have we identified to support this area of provision?
- Have we explored the full range of mainstream and external funding options available to us, including:
  - TECs?
  - Employment Training?
  - Task Force?
  - Education Support Grants?
  - ALBSU (Adult Literacy and Basic Skills Unit) grants?
- Have we conducted a community language needs analysis and identified local demographic and labour market trends for the purpose of targeting and strategic planning in this area?
- Have we developed an active language policy which addresses the needs of specific groups in the community (e.g. bilingual adults, refugees)?
- Are all potential students of ESOL offered appropriate pre-course guidance?
- Is our language support provision mapped to provide valid routes into employment or other learning opportunities?
- Have we fully researched those areas of employment where bilingualism is a prerequisite? How is this reflected in vocational provision available to bilingual adults?
- Is our language policy supported by a comprehensive programme of staff development aimed at both ESOL and subject specialists?

MODEL LANGUAGE POLICY

- Language provision will be based on an ongoing and carefully monitored analysis of the needs and wishes of the local population.

- Each student will receive a diagnosis of his/her language skills in academic, occupational and social contexts; and a statement of his/her progression options.

- Each course will provide a statement of the language skills necessary for its successful completion.

- Language tuition appropriate to the level and skills of all enrolled students will be provided.

- Language tuition will be complementary to the course of study it accompanies and, wherever possible, integrated within that course of study.

- The development of a computerised database of language support materials, cross-referenced by subject, communication skill and language function will be prioritised.

- Language support classes will be accredited or certificated in order to provide students with clearly identified progression routes.

- Tutors will be required to keep a record of individual students' progress, based on a combination of tutor and learner assessment.

(Based on the recommendations in *Bilingual Adults in Education and Training*, HMI Report, 1992.)

LANGUAGE FOR LEARNING

People from many different social, educational, cultural and linguistic backgrounds come to our education establishments, most of which are committed to an equal opportunities policy. This means ensuring that all students have access to the curriculum and the right to progression.

Language is central to learning because it is used in the formulation and communication of ideas, opinions and how we make sense of the world. In addition, it is also a means of cultural expression.

Language is a powerful medium. It can be used and is used to oppress, exclude, marginalise and limit the opportunities of some people while maximising the opportunities of others.

Who are the students in a class?

In a classroom, there is likely to be a range of varieties of English and of language spoken amongst the group. This is a resource in the class. Do not make any assumptions about why the students are in your class – other than to learn.

Social and Educational Context

Language is an integral part of the personal, social, class and cultural identity of a person.

There are many varieties of English e.g. Caribbean English, Irish English, London working-class English, Nigerian English, BBC English. In addition, because of colonialism, English is spoken in many parts of the world and most English speakers are bi or trilingual. Britain is a multilingual society. Over 170 languages are spoken in London.

Assumptions about a person's intelligence and personality are often made from the way s/he speaks. This is because society gives a different status to different varieties of English. For example, BBC English is generally invested with a higher status than London working-class English, both by people in positions of power and the speakers themselves. Equal opportunities policies require that we do not give this system of prejudice and discrimination any currency.

Some students are bilingual or multilingual. Some of these students are in the process of learning English and this process is temporary. Difficulty with English is no reflection of a student's ability. Therefore we must look for meaning in student's spoken and written contributions.

Figure 3.10 Extract from Language for Learning. One of a set of leaflets from Wandsworth Adult College

Lesson Planning

You will need to find out about the language skills of the students and look at them in conjunction with the language demands of the course. You will then be in a position to select strategies that enable all students to participate and have access to learning opportunities.

In addition, you will need to monitor your own use of language so that the subject matter is clear. Therefore don't use language which is above students' heads but avoid being patronising.

In the Classroom

- Learn the names of your students and how to pronounce them.
- Different cultures teach and learn in different ways. No one way is better than another, but your way may not be what students expect. Negotiate and discuss with the class the teaching methods that you will be using and what will be expected of the students.
- Tell students clearly what the objectives of the lesson are and how the lesson relates to the course.
- Discuss the language demands of the course with students openly.
- Create a safe environment where participation of all students in group discussions can realistically be encouraged. Students who are in the process of learning English frequently express diffidence about speaking in a large group because they think they might make grammar mistakes, people might not understand them or laugh at their English. Students must feel that the meaning of their contribution will be valued. A relaxed student learns more effectively and quickly and will keep in touch with any difficulties they are experiencing.
- If some students find intensive listening difficult, back up listening with visuals, use plain English and avoid colloquialisms and unnecessary digressions.
- Look for non-verbal communication e.g. gestures. Remember that there are different patterns of body language in different cultures.
- Take action if students talk or behave in a way that excludes others.

Devising a Course

Since language is so central to learning, every teacher is responsible for language in the classroom. This means identifying the language demands of the course and planning appropriate teaching methods.

Figure 3.10 (continued)

To determine the language demands of a course, ask yourself 'What reading, writing, speaking and listening skills will I be expecting of students?'

Here are some examples:

Teaching methods – language demands

Group discussion:
- participation by speaking
- intensive listening
- interjecting

Lecture/teacher presentation/demonstration:
- intensive listening
- note taking
- vocabulary
- language and confidence to ask and answer questions

Practical session:
- understand spoken/written instructions
- language and confidence to ask questions and ask for assistance

Access to learning and providing support

Group discussion:
- create opportunities for all students to participate
- use notes on board as back up

Lecture/teacher presentation/demonstration:
- sign posting e.g. 'I'm now going to talk about...', 'This is important...'
- check understanding of key vocabulary
- use key vocabulary in tasks
- repeat important points
- give notes (use bilingual notes if appropriate)

Practical session:
- demonstrate task
- provide written instructions (bilingual if appropriate)
- provide a list of ways to ask for assistance

Figure 3.10 (continued)

Resources

Bilingual Adults in Education and Training
HMI Report, 1992

Language in Education
FEU-NATECLA, 1989

Language, Learning and Race
FEU, 1987

English for Speakers of Other Languages: A programme for action
ALBSU, 1989

See also Language and Literacy Unit: Reports and Publications,
May 1992 for comprehensive resource list

ALBSU newsletters and publications

Useful Contacts

Adult Literacy and Basic Skills Unit (ALBSU), Kingsbourne House,
229–231 High Holborn, London WC1V 7DA. Tel: 071 405 4017

National Association of Teachers of English and Community
Languages (NATECLA), c/o NATECLA Administrator, Hall Green
College, 520–524 Stratford Rd, Birmingham B11 4AJ

Language and Literacy Unit, Southwark College, Gervase Street,
London SE15 2RJ. Tel: 071 639 9512

3.6 WORKING WITH REFUGEES

The accelerated growth of refugee communities in recent years has posed education and training providers at all levels with the challenge of responding to the very specific needs of peoples who have been uprooted and displaced. Although their circumstances are complex and determined by a diversity of ethnic, cultural and religious backgrounds, refugees have a number of common characteristics, many of which are evident, though less concentrated, in other black communities.

The number and origin of refugees varies widely around the country, but regardless of how they are dispersed, the implications for adult education providers and voluntary agencies that are working to alleviate their conditions are considerable.

Refugee students are likely to require specific educational responses, to take account of:

- disorientation resulting from the loss of close and extended family support and the adjustment to surviving alone
- desperate personal and financial circumstances, including the threat of deportation
- poor concentration and anxiety affecting assessment and classroom performance
- an impatience with irrelevant syllabi, inappropriate language support or lengthy progression routes which fail to offer short-term solutions
- lack of evidence of qualifications gained overseas, and the failure of many institutions to recognise them
- constant movement in and out of classes, due to displacement, homelessness or restrictions on concessionary fees
- different progression rates, due to differing levels of literacy, English competence and vocational or professional training
- the need for targeted ESOL provision, including intensive language courses, courses for academic purposes, bridging courses, professional bilingual skills training, etc.
- the absence of bilingual tutors, counsellors and guidance workers with relevant languages

- the different legal status of refugees and asylum-seekers, affecting grant eligibility, concessionary fees and other educational entitlements
- the need to study part-time in order to avoid overseas fees or pursue employment
- the lack of grant support to complete graduate and post-graduate studies which may have been suddenly interrupted
- the absence of appropriate referral systems and support networks, to provide welfare advice and advocacy services and thus alleviate pressure on language tutors.

A number of institutions, already faced with diminishing resources and organisational changes, have been unable or unwilling to develop rational, long-term, strategic responses aimed at reducing lengthening waiting lists for ESOL provision, and supporting the work of tutors and volunteers by funding essential mother-tongue counselling, guidance and assessment. This has contributed to a sense of siege in many areas where the concentrations of refugees are highest.

Where good practice with refugees has been developed, it has often resulted from the commitment of individual tutors, the efforts of refugees themselves, and on collaborative partnerships that draw on the skills and expertise of both. It has also been characterised by life-related teaching, which develops from the needs and experiences of the students; the training and employment of bi-lingual workers (often refugees themselves) to provide language and other specialist support services; the provision of discrete, tailor-made language courses to meet identified refugee needs; and the availability of personal, financial, welfare and childcare support.

WORKING WITH REFUGEES

Issues for Refugee Students

- Am I capable of studying after what I've been through? Will the trauma, anxiety and dislocation I feel affect my ability to concentrate?
- What is the quickest route to qualification and/or employment so that I can support myself and my family?
- What skills, prior experience or qualifications do I have? Can I use or develop them to help me survive here?
- How well can I communicate in English in social, occupational or academic settings?
- What are my learning priorities? Will I be expected to spend time learning English first?
- How does the education system work in this country? Can I get advice in my own language on how to negotiate it?
- What level of language support is most appropriate for me? Is a suitable class available in this area?
- Can I follow a vocational course at the same time as improving my written or spoken English skills?
- Will my housing, family or refugee status prevent me from completing the course? If I have to move from the area, will I have to start again from scratch?
- How long will it take me to achieve my desired goal? Can I do an intensive or bridging course to speed up the process?
- Can I afford to study? What registration or examination fees am I expected to pay? Will there be additional travel, childcare or equipment costs?
- What grant support, concessionary fees or income support am I entitled to? How and where do I apply?
- Can I use my bilingual skills to assist other refugees from my country or to help me get a job?

WORKING WITH REFUGEES

Issues for Practitioners

- What do we need to know about refugee students in order to give relevant advice and assistance?
- Will our questions and style of interview or assessment appear intrusive, interrogational or insensitive? How can we avoid this?
- Do we really need to establish residential and immigration status, ask to see passports, official documents, etc.? Is this an appropriate role (would it be sufficient to ask only for evidence of Income Support)?
- Do we mistake depression, anxiety, poor concentration or poor English communication skills for incompetence? Do our assessment methods take account of the effects of personal trauma?
- Have we conducted a needs analysis of ESOL students and refugees?
- How can we make the classes and teaching resources we have developed for non-refugee groups more appropriate?
- Are we aware of cultural, religious and political differences in the classroom? Do we exacerbate them in any way?
- Can we target language provision so that it meets the campaigning needs of refugee communities (e.g. presenting views, arguing case for support, organising information seminars, etc.)?
- How effective is our liaison with subject or specialist tutors?
- Have we developed complementary learning resources and integrated assignments to complement vocational courses?
- Have we identified appropriate progression routes? Are there any avoidable delays, hurdles or requirements?

WORKING WITH REFUGEES

Issues for Managers

- What resources have we identified to support this expanding area of work?
- Have we explored all available funding options, including those available via the voluntary sector?
- Have we explored all other potential partnerships, including collaboration with refugee organisations, voluntary organisations, social services, religious groups, campaign groups?
- Do we collaborate with other education and training providers to ensure that local refugee provision is rationalised?
- Have we explored possible teaching partnerships with other agencies and/or refugee communities?
- Have we conducted a local needs analysis and developed a strategic plan with other agencies in response to the identified needs of local refugees?
- Have we developed a co-ordinated, cross-institutional response to the needs of refugee students?
- Have we explored ways of establishing tailor-made courses for different groups of refugees (e.g. childminders' course for Eritrean women, catering course for Vietnamese, bilingual business course, etc.)?
- Where are the majority of refugee students concentrated? Are they ghettoised because of a lack of appropriate language support for students on mainstream courses?
- Do we plan for double staffing on courses which attract bilingual students?
- Do we have a concessionary fees policy for refugee students?
- Do staff have access to relevant training in interviewing, assessment, accreditation, cross-cultural counselling, etc.?

WHAT DO REFUGEES HAVE IN COMMON?

A high percentage of refugees:

- are young and single (i.e. arrived in this country alone)
- are professionally qualified or well-educated (although not necessarily via English)
- are highly motivated and determined to learn fast
- are mothers of young children
- have already acquired formal English

Almost all refugees:

- have been through terrifying and traumatising experiences
- have lost close relatives or have relatives who are missing or in prison
- have had bad interrogational experiences with officials
- are anxious or guilty about those they have left behind
- constantly think about and long to go home
- are significantly poorer since arriving in Britain
- face long-term unemployment (refugees face the highest rates of unemployment in the country)
- hate being dependent
- are unable to pay fees for courses or examinations
- are told daily that they are not wanted here

(With thanks to Marion Molteno of Croydon ESOL Service, who provided this list.)

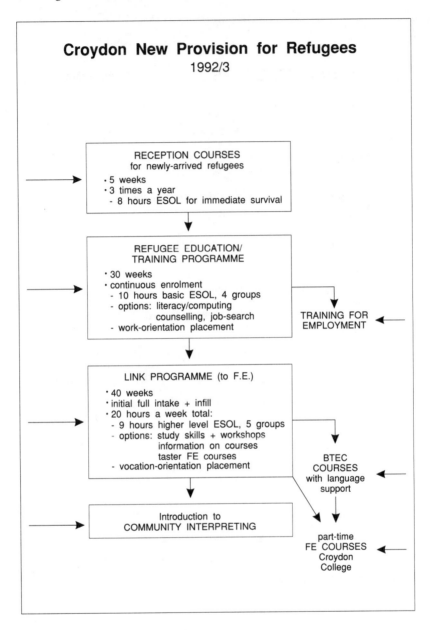

Figure 3.11 Outline of a Model of Provision for Refugees in Croydon

JOB LIFELINE FOR REFUGEES

Unique career help launched for professionals

▪ REPORT BY CAROL HASSALL

A TRAIL-blazing scheme to improve the quality of life for hundreds of refugees is being set up in Birmingham.

And if the pioneering initiative is successful, it could be adopted all over the country by next year.

Jenny Warmington, a former lecturer in English at Bournville College of Further Education is taking on a group of refugees from places such as Yugoslavia, China, Sudan and Chile and giving them a helping hand getting back into their professions.

Her project is causing such a stir in the refugee community, she is having enquiries from as far away as London.

The aim of the scheme is to help professional people, who have fled from their native countries, pick up their working life in Birmingham with language help and an assessment of how their qualifications stand here.

"It was recognised there was a real problem for professional refugees coming over here," said Jenny.

"It was primarily a language problem but also difficulties with whether their qualifications counted or not.

"My role is to give guidance and support and once they have completed a 10 to 12 week course they have a lot more confidence.

"They are really just glad I'm here and all the people I've met so far think it's a great idea. I feel very good being able to help."

Jenny is currently waiting for a grant from the Department of Education and Science to fund a research post to monitor her group's progress.

Anyone wanting help can contact Jenny on 411 1414 ext 239.

Figure 3.12 Local newspaper story about Bournville College Refugee Project

Figure 3.12 (continued) Bournville College Refugee Project course publicity

138

ACCREDITATION AND RECOGNITION OF REFUGEE PROFESSIONAL QUALIFICATION, SUPPORT & GUIDANCE PROJECT

What is Accreditation and Recognition of Overseas Qualifications?

Accreditation of Prior Learning is a way of obtaining credits for what you can already do. If you have a Degree from Zaire for example, you should not have to complete a course of 3 years for the same degree in the UK, but instead, be allowed credits for the qualification you already have. In this way, you will receive exemptions from a full course and so accelerate the process of obtaining UK recognition of your qualifications.

This project is designed to examine the issues involved and to take individuals through a process of development to enable them to continue their professional careers in this country.

Entry Requirements

The Project is open to any refugee who is professionally qualified and who is currently experiencing difficulty in either getting those qualifications accepted in the UK or is prevented from being able to use those qualifications because of lack of English communication skills.

Why is the Project different?

It is designed especially for refugees with professional qualifications.

It is not a formal course. We will try to make programmes as individual as possible and we hope that within every 10-12 week period, we will be able to work with 10 different people.

What do I study?

If you should require it, English Language support is available and if it is necessary, we will try to make it as specific to a professional area as possible.

We may also be looking to place you on a short term work placement where you are assessed in what you can do, or we may be looking at short intensive courses run at Higher Education Institutions.

What does this process lead to?

UK recognition of professional qualifications held by refugees.

If I'm interested what should I do?

Ring the **Project Manager - Jenny Warmington -** on
021 411 1414 ext 239
or any of the Refugee Agencies:-

Midland Refugee Council
Ockenden Venture
Midland Vietnamese Association
Refugee Action

Figure 3.12 (continued)

Resources

Refugee Education Handbook
WUS, 1989
(invaluable and comprehensive guide to educational resources and agencies working with refugees.)

International Guide to Qualifications
Mansell

Cultural Aspects of Job-hunting
Tony Marshall, Refugee Council, 1989

Refugee Education Policy for the 1990s
Refugee Education and Training Working Group, Refugee Council, 1990

Useful Contacts

World University Service, Refugee Education Advisory Service, 20 Compton Terrace, London N1 2UN. Tel: 071 226 6747

Refugee Council, 3 Bondway, London SW8. Tel: 071 582 6922

Refugee Employment Training, 240–250 Ferndale Rd, Brixton, London SW9 8BB. Tel: 071 737 1155

Africa Educational Trust, 38 King Street, London WC2E 8JS. Tel: 071 836 5075

United Kingdom Council on Overseas Student Affairs (UKCOSA), 60 Westbourne Grove, London W2 5SH. Tel: 071 229 9268/9

United Kingdom Immigrants Advisory Service (UKIAS), Refugee Unit, County House, 2nd Floor, 190 Great Dover Street, London SE1 4YB. Tel: 071 357 7421

Midland Refugee Council, c/o Race Relations Unit, Chief Executive's Department, Council House, Birmingham B1 1BB. Tel: 021 235 2575

North-East Refugee Service, c/o Citizens Advice Bureau, 5 Regents Terrace, Gateshead, Tyne and Wear, NE8 1HH. Tel: 091 490 0314

Northern Refugee Centre, Jew Lane, Off Fitzalan Square, Sheffield S1 2BE

Oxfordshire Refugee Council, East Oxford Community Centre, 44B Princess Street, Oxford OX4 1DD. Tel: 0865 790490

West Yorkshire Refugee Service, c/o Save the Children, UK North and East Divisional Office, 2nd Floor, National Deposit House, 1 Eastgate, Leeds LS2 7L

APPENDIX 1 RACE EQUALITY TERMS:
Some Useful Definitions

WAYS OF DESCRIBING PEOPLE

BLACK ... is the general term used throughout this book to refer to those who, because of their race, colour or ethnic origin, are visibly identifiable as different from the ethnic majority. The term encompasses people from a wide range of communities with huge cultural, social, linguistic, religious and, in some cases, political differences, and includes third- or fourth-generation African-Caribbeans and Asians, as well as refugees from Vietnam, Somalia or Uganda.

Some would argue that it denies these differences and fails to acknowledge the importance of people's national identity. It is nevertheless a convenient way of emphasising black people's shared experience as identifiable targets and victims of racism, with its common roots in the history of slavery and/or colonialism. It also helps to remind us of the common anti-racist strategies and political responses which are needed to combat it. Most important of all, it is a term with which most black people identify, once they recognise that it refers to a shared political experience rather than to skin tone.

BILINGUAL ... adults are those who use two or more languages in their daily lives. They may not be fluent in English and may therefore need ESOL (English as a Second or Other Language) classes to improve their spoken or written command of the language. They should not be referred to as 'ESOL students', however, but as science or GCSE students who need language support.

REFUGEES ... are defined by the 1951 United Nations convention as those with a 'well-founded fear of persecution' in his or her native country 'for reasons of race, religion, nationality or membership of a particular social group or political opinion'.

ASYLUM-SEEKERS ... are people awaiting a decision on their application for refugee status. Increasingly since 1980, they have been granted 'exceptional leave to remain', which is something less than full refugee status. They are required to renew their right to stay regularly, but after seven years they are usually granted 'indefinite leave to remain'.

COLOURED ... is generally considered to be a derogatory term, because it ignores the fact that everyone has coloured skin pigmentation, and assumes that whiteness is the norm with which everyone who is not white should be compared. It is particularly offensive because of its associations with the Apartheid system in South Africa, which classifies the non-white population as blacks, Indians or 'coloureds' – and, above all, it is not the word black people would choose to describe themselves.

PEOPLE OF COLOUR ... is the umbrella term used in the United States to refer to descendants of (non-white) immigrant and slave communities such as African-Americans, Puerto Ricans and Vietnamese. For the reasons given above (see 'coloured') it has not caught on here.

HALF-CASTE ... is also considered a negative term. It implies that the person being described is in some way inadequate or incomplete and, like mulatto (originally a Spanish term for a cross between an ass and a mule), it ignores national identity.

MIXED RACE ... is nowadays the term preferred by most people of mixed parentage, because it highlights the race factor - and hence the racism – which invariably affects their lives. Many people of mixed race also choose to identify themselves as black (because one white parent makes no difference to a racist); or by their parents' nationality (e.g. Anglo-Nigerian, Afro-British, etc.).

IMMIGRANT ... is a term to be avoided, because the vast majority of black young people could not, by any stretch of the imagination, be described as immigrants. It ignores the fact that nearly half of all black people in this country were born here – and that more than half of those who emigrated to Britain have been here for 15 or more years. When used in the media, it rarely includes white immigrants (for example, people from Australia, Canada or South Africa), and has often been used to inflame fears about so-called immigrants 'swamping' British culture.

ETHNIC MINORITY ... continues to be used by many officials and institutions, particularly in ethnic monitoring exercises and published documents. However, some black people reject the term because it includes the many white 'ethnic minorities' in the UK who, whilst experiencing discrimination on the grounds of language or religion, do not experience racial disadvantage due to their colour. Apart from marginalising racism in this way, the term has negative, bureaucratic associations with 'ethnic' neediness. It also emphasises the power relationship of the white majority over the black minorities in this country, overlooking the fact that in global terms, it is in fact white people who are in the minority.

WAYS OF DESCRIBING ATTITUDES AND BEHAVIOUR

RACISM ... is often described as 'prejudice plus power'. However, this is a simplistic definition, since it implies that only people in obvious power or authority can be racist. In fact, racism describes a complex set of attitudes and behaviour towards another racial or ethnic group, with very distinct historical origins in the 'pseudo-scientific' (and now discredited) beliefs about race that developed in Europe during the eighteenth and nineteenth centuries, based on:

the belief that differences in physical or cultural characteristics (such as skin colour, language, dress, religious practices, etc.) correspond directly to differences in personality, intelligence or ability

the social and economic power of members of one racial or ethnic group to enforce and enact such attitudes and behaviour towards others.

INSTITUTIONAL RACISM ... refers to those procedures and practices within an organisation or institution which support and encourage direct or indirect racial discrimination.

ANTI-RACISM ... is the conscious endeavour to challenge and combat racism in all its behavioural and institutional forms.

MULTI-CULTURALISM ... is the belief that many different cultures should be encouraged and allowed to flourish in society, and that services and facilities such as health, education, the arts, etc. should be delivered in a way that embodies and promotes this belief.

PREJUDICE ... is, literally, pre-judging people in a negative way according to pre-conceived ideas or stereotypes of them.

STEREOTYPING ... is making broad generalisations about particular groups of people and expecting all members of that group to think and behave identically.

RACIAL HARASSMENT ... refers to intentional acts of verbal or physical abuse or threatening behaviour towards people of another racial or ethnic group. It includes name-calling, the use of abusive language and (in its most extreme form) acts of racially-motivated violence.

DIRECT DISCRIMINATION ... is treating people less favourably on the grounds of race, nationality, religion, gender, etc. (N.B. The Race Relations and Sex Discrimination Acts make this illegal in the United Kingdom.)

INDIRECT DISCRIMINATION ... is applying a rule or requirement which effectively leads to less favourable conditions or treatment for a particular group of people.

POSITIVE DISCRIMINATION ... is treating people more favourably on the grounds of race, nationality, religion, gender, etc. in order to redress the disadvantages arising from their experience of discrimination (for example in employment or education).

POSITIVE ACTION ... is offering special help to people who are disadvantaged because of prejudice, stereotyping and discrimination so that they can take full and equal advantage of opportunities in jobs, education, training, services, etc. This is not illegal, and special provision is made for positive action in the relevant Acts.

AFFIRMATIVE ACTION ... is a term commonly used in the United States to refer to positive discrimination.

GHETTOISATION ... refers to the process by which black people are confined to services and areas of provision which are low-level, second-rate or poorly resourced, or which attract a disproportionately large black clientele for the wrong reasons.

SOME OTHER USEFUL TERMS

ETHNICITY ... is a distinctive sense of cultural and historical identity based on belonging by birth to a particular cultural group.

ETHNOCENTRICITY ... is viewing the world from the perspective of a particular ethnic group, often with the assumption that the values, beliefs and achievements of that group are superior to those of other ethnic groups. Eurocentric assumptions, for example, are at the root of much of what is learnt in the school curriculum. All groups have the ability to be ethnocentric – and for people descended from Africa, it has been necessary to adopt an Afrocentric approach to the study of history, art, literature and other aspects of black achievement, simply to redress their invisibility.

NATIONALISM ... is a distinctive sense of cultural and historical identity and/or common destiny based on being a citizen of a particular nation state. In its most extreme forms, such as Nazism or Apartheid, it has resulted in acts of genocide or 'ethnic cleansing', justified by a belief in the natural superiority of the aggressor. In Britain, it has given rise to groups like the National Front and the British National Party.

THIRD WORLD ... refers to non-industrialised countries outside Europe and America. The term is increasingly challenged by those who object to its third-rate, third-rank connotations. Some prefer to say 'the two-thirds world', arguing that terms like 'third world', 'developing' or 'under-developed' are patronising and Eurocentric.

About the Author

Stella Dadzie was formerly Head of Educational Guidance at Haringey College (now the College of North East London).

She has 15 years' experience as a black teacher, lecturer, student counsellor and manager in further education, working with 'marginalised' groups, including the unemployed, women and black adults.

She is co-author of *The Heart of the Race: Black women's lives in Britain*, which won the Martin Luther King Award for Literature in 1986. She is currently a freelance training consultant for Front Line Training, specialising in equal opportunities, race equality, guidance and other issues. She has worked for NIACE, REPLAN and FATEBU on a number of projects concerning black adult learners.

Among her other publications for NIACE are *Educational Guidance with Black Communities: A checklist of good practice* (1990), *Essential Skills for Race Equality Trainers* (1992) and the *Survey of Numbers of Black Adults with Professional Qualifications Gained Overseas* (1993).